NOBODY MOVED YOUR CHEESE!

How to Ignore the "Experts"...and Trust Your Gut.

By Ross Shafer

Printed in Victoria, Canada

National Library of Canada Cataloguing in Publication Data

Shafer, Ross
    Nobody moved your cheese! / Ross Shafer.
ISBN 1-55395-658-3
    I. Title.
BF637.S8S49 2003   158.1   C2003-
900358-2

TRAFFORD

This book was published *on-demand* in cooperation with Trafford Publishing.
On-demand publishing is a unique process and service of making a book available for retail sale to the public taking advantage of on-demand manufacturing and Internet marketing. **On-demand publishing** includes promotions, retail sales, manufacturing, order fulfilment, accounting and collecting royalties on behalf of the author.

Suite 6E, 2333 Government St., Victoria, B.C. V8T 4P4, CANADA
Phone   250-383-6864   Toll-free 1-888-232-4444 (CA & US)
Fax   250-383-6804   E-mail sales@trafford.com
Web site   www.trafford.com
TRAFFORD PUBLISHING IS A DIVISION OF TRAFFORD HOLDINGS LTD.
Trafford Catalogue #03-0021   www.trafford.com/robots/03-0021.html

10   9   8   7   6   5   4

THE CHAPTERS

PAGE

Fighting Words? (a so-called introduction)

THE EXPERTS ARE WRONG ABOUT YOU

YOUR JOB IS TERMINAL...& OTHER GOOD NEWS

DEDICATION

This book is for Leah. She is my best friend and my full time *Muse*. (I hope I'm hers) She makes me laugh harder and more often than anybody I've ever known. Beyond that, I am eternally grateful and honored to be her husband. I love her more than I can express on paper.

Thank you, sweetheart.

Nobody Moved Your Cheese!

ACKNOWLEDGMENTS

I have a lot of people to thank for letting me live this interesting life. From time to time they have gifted me with their inspiration, anger, insight, frustration, joy, indifference, wisdom, ignorance, sadness, and empathy. I promise to repay each of them, with either generosity or vengeance. *(They'll know I'm kidding about which half of that I mean)* First, I have to thank my funny and kind mother and father, Chuck and Lois. Thank you to my exceedingly handsome and intelligent sons, Adam and Ryan. Also to my brothers Clell and Scott and their families. And I cannot forget my great and interesting friends, Kelly Monteith, Jim Sharp, Bill Nye, Doug & Ronell Gall, Mort & Kenslea Sahl, John Powell, Mike & Wanda Bevan, John Keister, John & Barbara Lloyd, Rand Rosenberg, Bill & Lynne Kirchenbauer, Tom Dreesen, Johnny & Susie Dark, Johnny & Angela Witherspoon, Drew & Trina Hedgcock, Wil Shriner, David Feldman, Jeff & Malinda Altman, Joe Griffith, Michael Burger, Paul and Marlise Boland, Peter Crabbe, Jann Karam, Jeff Patterson, Steve Oedekerk, Fred Wolf, Bruce Feirstein, Chip Hanauer, John Cramer, Mike and Kristin Dimich, Howard Papush and Tim Mason, Joe Applebaum, Brian Kaufman, and all of the people I've been in business with who've maintained their integrity and followed through on their promises; to me and to others. And of course, to Lee and Cheryl Dale...and the entire Dale family *(there is a wonderful gaggle of them)* for making me a part of your amazingly loving clan.

Oh and *God*, most of all, *YOU*. You're the real deal!

Ross Shafer   7

FIGHTING WORDS?

How dare I challenge you to ignore the advice of your friends, your family and your loved ones? What gives me the right to encourage you to question the wisdom of relationship Diva, Dr. Laura, or the motivational maven, Tony Robbins, or even the former field general of GE, Jack Welch? Worse, how could I possibly pick on the nice man whose asked millions of people worldwide the question, *"Who Moved Your Cheese?"*

Because I think these so called "experts" are dead wrong about what *they* think is right for YOU. Only YOU know what's right for YOU.

As a TV & radio host, I've interviewed the usual suspects of popular authors, experts and pundits. As a speaker and entertainer, I've shared the podium with a lot of them. Most of these professional advice-dispensers are hawking a best selling book, a survey, or a 10-step formula they claim will dramatically change YOUR life. You and I could probably choke a library with the copies we've bought. Then, if you're like me, you've missed your favorite sitcoms studying; dutifully attempting to emulate their success. But their books, surveys and formulas don't exactly apply to You. Only *You* apply to You.

Besides, the experts don't know you. They don't know your employer, your stockholders or your family dynamics. They don't share your dreams or have experienced your roadblocks. Fact is, they probably don't care if you succeed or fail.

That's YOUR job. Because it's YOUR life!

So, stop listening to the "Experts" and TRUST YOUR OWN GUT. In the end, It's ALWAYS about YOU!

CHAPTER 1

EVERYBODY IS WRONG... *EXCEPT YOU!*

First, I need you to follow two important rules.

#1   For the duration of this book, promise me you will remain totally self-absorbed.

#2   Make the assumption that *Everybody* is wrong and that *You* are right.   I am especially referring to the people who have told you, to your face, that you *couldn't* do something you wanted to do.

Have you ever heard those words and then vowed to prove that person wrong? If you have, then you bought the right book.

I used to hear those words all the time.

When I was working as an unhappy pet shop manager, I told people I wanted to become a comedian and talk show host;

just like Johnny Carson. Everyone thought I was absolutely insane. They said I had NO chance. Said I wasn't funny enough. Said I didn't have any "connections." Said I should be happy scooping pet poop for a living. They had the current facts right but each one of them was dead wrong about me. The same goes for you. Nobody knows what You are capable of; except You.

And I'm even talking about the people who insist they know and love you! Your parents, your relatives, your siblings, your friends, and your work mates (especially your boss) all love to give you advice about your career, your friends, your lovers, the kinds of food you eat, your taste in clothing, the furniture you buy, the medicine you take, the music you like, the pets you own, the hobbies you choose, the alcohol you guzzle, the secret vices you don't think they know...and the list only gets longer, right? Why do they do this? Because they all think of themselves as "experts" who have "been through it before" and know what's good for YOU. Sound familiar?

What about the "published experts" who worm their way into your psyche? The talk show guests and leaders of your industry who sell you books and cite their case studies to back up their claims. They have "proof" that they know how you can do your job better, make more money, be a better salesperson, a stronger leader, a better parent, and ultimately, how to achieve bliss and eternal happiness.

They're wrong about you, too!

Have you read their books and followed their hallowed advice even though it didn't feel right to you? That's because, down deep, you didn't believe it. I'll bet you soon lost interest or got too busy with your life. We usually don't lose interest in things that feel right to us. In fact, we usually can't get enough of them.

Again, *you* were right and *they* were wrong.

You are the one who has to live with your decisions; not the experts. You are the one who suffers the consequences and enjoys the victories. So, I think this book will be worth the cover price if you eventually put it away and trust your own instincts. Rely on your own gut feelings. Listen to your own inner guide. As a religious person I think the gnawing in your stomach is God nudging you. Even the non-religious folks must admit that "to thine own self be true" is a pretty relevant credo.

Oh, you'll make mistakes. You'll make plenty of errors in judgement. That's deliciously human. But in doing so, you will have practiced EXTREME responsibility. You will have proven you could be accountable to yourself. You reconciled, with yourself, to live with your decision before you made it. That is being right-minded.

And, <u>that</u> is never wrong.

So as you're reading, challenge the old conventions. Challenge the experts and their "proven formulas." Most importantly, challenge yourself to trust yourself. It's much easier (and faster) to make decisions when the first person you ask for advice is...*You.*

So here we go. The first thing you need to know is...

THE

"EXPERTS"

ARE

WRONG

ABOUT

YOU.

CHAPTER 2

NOBODY MOVED YOUR CHEESE.

A friend of mine asked, "Ross, what does *my* cheese have to do with anything?"

Well, for the uninitiated, the reference point is Spencer Johnson's worldwide best seller, *Who Moved My Cheese?* There is even a popular animated training movie of the same name. The video tells the story of two cute little mice who have been eating cheese from the same stockpile, for years. Then, one day they wake up and their cheese is gone. Is this boring you?

Bear with me.

Spencer's book isn't about mice, at all. It's about YOU and how well you adapt to change. See, these mice are living a fat and happy life until they wake up to discover their cheese is missing. If the mice don't venture off and look for new cheese (adapt to change), they will surely starve to death.

This is supposed to be very bad. But, bad for who? You? Or the organization that wants you to change? If your gut tells you following the new cheese trail isn't right, you don't have to adapt. Instead, you have at least three options. (1) Learn how to maintain your integrity and grow with your current employer. (2) Do what you do with a different company. (3) Strike out on your own.

Most of the executives I've talked to prefer the first option.

The people I've met (who've bolted for bigger potential and better working conditions) say they regret their early departure and would urge you to, "Stay where you are and make your current cheese work." In fact, many of those who left for greener pastures were "put out to pasture" because they compromised their integrity.

I know plenty of "mice" who don't want to look for new cheese. In fact, they think looking for new cheese might just be a "mouse trap." (You have no idea how long I've waited to turn that phrase.)

If you think the grass is greener elsewhere, you're wrong. You'll have to start over making contacts, learning the systems, and wasting your time evading the political potholes created by your arrival. Beyond that, your old problems might end up stalking you at your new location. Hang onto your cheese.

You all know the pop singer, Sting. His former manager, Miles Copeland (brother to *The Police's* Stuart Copeland), is a very successful music producer. Miles told me that his friend and client Pat McDonald (who wrote the song, *The Future's So Bright I Gotta Wear Shades*) has been offered more than 4 million dollars to sell that song for use in TV commercials. But Pat won't take the money. Patrick is not a rich man, and could probably use the money, but he flatly refuses to sell out his art for a buck - not even for 4 million of them. He likes his cheese right where it is. Cheese, in this case, equals Pat's integrity.

My friend, Mike Neun, is also a great example of a guy who wasn't seduced by the prospect of lucrative new cheese.

Mike is one of the funniest, most prolific, low-key comedians I know. Mike says, "My friends want me to go deer hunting but I don't like hunting. Oh, I love the killing. It's the camaraderie and walking around in the woods that I hate." He's appeared on several network television shows and was offered a starring role in his own TV show. All Mike had to do was wear a tuxedo and trade barbs with the 24-piece orchestra leader every night.

Mike tried, but found out his conscience wouldn't allow it.

He hates tuxedos and phony banter. He couldn't even fake it. It just wasn't in him. The cheese brokers had moved a huge pile of cheese too far from his comfort zone. So, he bailed and has lived happily ever after on a beautiful teak sailboat named Watauga. Mike claims Watauga is the Indian word for, "varnish all summer."

If you get a chance, rent the movie, *Life as a House* starring Kevin Kline. You won't allow anyone to move your cheese, ever again.

Kevin plays a respected architect who takes painstaking pride in his detailed scale models. However, his company wants him to stop making models and learn the CAD computer assisted drawing program. Instead, Kevin won't compromise and quits to build his dream home, instead. The home becomes a wonderful metaphor for his life.

I've had my own cheese moved a few times. I had a great job with an advertising agency. Big money. Prestige. One day, the boss announced he wanted to give me an even bigger raise. All I would have to do was to start "double billing" the clients for advertising. Some of them would catch the mistake and squawk. Others wouldn't pay attention and just pay the bill. In either case, according to my boss, we could always blame the accounting department for the error. My stomach ached. I couldn't sleep. Ultimately, I couldn't go through with it. My boss moved the cheese too far from my integrity. I had to quit in order to find less sickening cheese, elsewhere.

We don't ALL have to robotically follow the moved cheese just because *they* say change is good.

As long as you live, you are worth more than WHAT you do. It is WHO you are that has lasting value. If WHO you are can't live with the change, then you have to have the courage of your convictions to stay true to yourself. If you are kind, conscientious, and skilled, you will easily find your own cheese; well within reach of your true character and hard-earned integrity.

IT'S ALWAYS ABOUT YOU:

Is what you want really over "there?" Or, do you feel obligated (yet uncomfortable) to follow the pack to the new pile of cheese? If so, why are you resisting the change? Does the change go against your principles? Against your core values? Against your high standards? Are you satisfied with your current career status but don't want to compromise? Then, don't. Make yourself happy somewhere else. But before you do, take a hard look at what you will have to do to achieve your current cheese status. Are you willing to take a few steps backward at first? Are you in an impossible situation or are you looking for a quick fix? Can't decide? If the decision is that close, stay where you are until you figure it all out.

Above all, don't let fear and worry paralyze you from what your gut tells you is right. With enough time, you'll be able to weigh all of the options. You will only feel unsure for a short time. Then, you will settle into knowing that you made the right decision.

And, we can all get some sleep.

CHAPTER 3

ANTHONY ROBBINS HASN'T DONE A DAMN THING!

If there was anyone who thinks he knows how to realize YOUR potential it is Anthony Robbins. You've seen him on TV and you may have even bought his books and tapes. But what has he done, really?

For one, he knows how to suck people in. I bought *Awaken The Giant Within* but fell asleep before I could finish it.

To me, he was an easy comic target. Those sappy motivational infomercials. That enormous head. That piano-key grin. Yes, I admit to sinking low enough to utter, "Anthony Robbins has so many teeth that when he got them capped, 47 people had to go on back order."

Or, this one. "Nobody is *that* optimistic. I have a feeling that if Tony Robbins ever went to jail he'd tell people he was living in a "gated community."

Well, the laugh was on me when I was told I was going to have to "follow him" at a major health industry conference. He was a last minute guest speaker and they shifted the program to suit his schedule. Gulp!

This guy is an imposing six feet seven inches tall and really, really loud! He storms the stage with a muscular body that contorts in such violent moves that the stage is quickly chewed up, spit out and every evangelist within 500 miles runs for cover. Tony's mighty fists pound the air as he hammers the audience into championing his amazing new "life technology." A "technology" that will transform anyone's life. The audience suspends common sense with every persuasive syllable. He promises to help make you thin, rich, powerful, a better parent, a more loving spouse, and the best friend anyone could have. It's the formula for an incredible life...and it's on sale today for an unprecedented low, low price!

I stood in the wings; dumfounded.

Anthony urged the riveted crowd to recognize and tap into their personal power. He encouraged them to improve their vocabulary, to mirror the success of others, and develop mastery in a single area of expertise. Rapt throngs of people cheer and cry and jump to their feet when he's done. He left the stage sweaty and spent.

As he blew by me, his monstrous smile blinded me. At the same time, I felt my right hand being swallowed by his giant, enveloping grip.

I was supposed to follow that?

The after-show autograph line (for Tony...not me) took forever to die down. As a performer, I really admired what he had just accomplished. But, as his presence wore off, I thought to myself, "Wait a sec. Tony Robbins hasn't done a damn thing." Tony hasn't built a revolutionary rapid transit system or a groundbreaking wireless technology or built a chain of retail stores from the ground up. He hasn't introduced a lifesaving medicine, changed the course of military history or even designed a better Kentucky Fried Chicken Spork. He got famous for selling tapes of himself on a TV show that HE paid for. The "technology" he touts is simply information and quotes he's gathered from successful people elsewhere. Yet, he commands amazingly high fees to consult with professional sports teams, captains of industry, and even leaders of countries.

He's a brilliant showman but he's not an original.

He's just louder!

Let me take an apropos side street. I met football great, Fran Tarkenton, in the early 90's when Fran was the host for Tony's first TV Infomercial. I asked Fran if this Anthony Robbins character was for real. Fran said, "Hey, he sells a lot of tapes." I pressed. "No, no Sir Francis. Don't snow me. *Why* does he sell all of those tapes?"

I'll never forget what Fran told me. "All I know is that he delivers passion. Tony is so passionate...believes in himself so much...and in what he's doing...that he radiates that passion to other people. The guy is a phenom!"

Fran was dead bang right. Tony Robbins was excited about being...Tony Robbins. And since most of us want the secret to success so badly, we'll follow anyone who thinks they know what and where it is. That is the power of having a passion for something. Passion rubs off. Passion moves people to spend money, leave home, change jobs, change wives, form an empire, and start a war. Yup, enthusiasm will carry you to your dream and beyond.

That's Tony Robbins trick. He has a way of getting people to become passionate about themselves! He hasn't accomplished anything in the tangible way we usually measure accomplishment. He hasn't done anything you can't do yourself. And, he hasn't told you anything the Army hasn't been telling you for years; "Be all you can be!" Tony just has longer commercials.

By the way, I WAS able to follow Tony Robbins on stage, that night. When I went out I said, "Man, I am so disappointed. That guy must have been listening to me rehearse in my dressing room. Because he just said exactly what I was going to say tonight (laugh) word-for-word! (Laugh) Now there's no way I am going to be able to sell all of those tapes in my car!"

IT'S ALWAYS ABOUT YOU:

So, what's YOUR passion? Are you able to memorize 30 years of baseball stats but forget the 6-item grocery list? Can you sing every song on the radio but you can't remember the new products in your latest sales brochure? Your memory isn't fading. You never have a bad memory for the subjects you're passionate for, do you? You'll also have plenty of energy and time when you commit yourself to your passions. Follow your passion and the happiness and money will take care of itself. Go on. Admit you love sports or knitting or pets or stereo gear or boating. Challenge yourself to make your passion pay the bills.

That will be *Your* technology.

CHAPTER 4

SWEAT THE SMALL STUFF... OR DIE!

If this is a shock to you, you are probably unemployed or on the way. Because if you don't sweat the small stuff, you'll have no place in this world; let alone a job!

I interviewed the author of those *Don't Sweat The Small Stuff* books, Richard Carlson, Ph.D., when I was hosting a local TV show in Seattle. I found him to be an ultra syrupy, sickeningly nice person who just made me ill. So sweet. So genuine. So sensitive. Afterward, I wanted to go out and buy cigars and porno to get my equilibrium back.

While these books are enormously successful, I think they're like getting a morphine drip for a shattered femur. They temporarily mask the pain but the injury is still there.

Now, I don't have a problem with Richard trying to get people to calm down, relax, put things in perspective, and not take the world so seriously. I completely agree, Doc. Way too many people die from road rage and mistreated ex-employees. But I laughed until milk shot out of my nose when he wrote the book, *Don't Sweat the Small Stuff...At Work.* I couldn't believe I was reading chapters like, *Don't Sweat the Bureaucracy, Don't Dramatize the Deadlines, Don't Sweat the Demanding Boss,* and *Dare to Be Happy.* Is he kidding?! Has Dr. Carlson ever punched a real time clock? And I don't count his psychologist "Your Time's-Up" alarm. Has he ever had to sweat a sixty-day employee evaluation? I'll bet not! He's a therapist who listens to your life, takes surveys of other people's lives, and writes books about them.

Since you don't have that luxury, don't get suckered by that book.

The small stuff is *all* you have to sweat. You were hired to be productive, to be innovative, to be collaborative, and to help the company turn a profit. You sold your soul to that corporate devil in return for a weekly paycheck! And now, somebody is telling you that you should have less small stuff to sweat? Dr. Carlson is on another planet if he thinks *your* personal well being, at work, takes precedent over the reason you were hired in the first place.

What's happened to us? We've become a nation of thin-skinned victims! My God, we live in a world where your company hires a trauma therapist if you get stuck in an elevator over the lunch hour. Except, the therapy is not to medicate your scarred psyche. It's to avoid a lawsuit. What ever happened to toughing it out? Sucking it up?

When I played football we knew the game was rough and we learned to play with a little pain. I know this firsthand because radio announcers would refer to me as "the guy who was shaken up on the play." Besides, why must we measure stress in terms of small stuff and big stuff? It's all just normal stuff that needs to be done to keep the company doors open and your camper payment from bouncing.

That would be like ME showing up to entertain 1,000 people and telling the agent, "Look, I'm feeling kinda edgy from the turbulence of my two-connection flight. So I am not going to sweat it if the audience doesn't laugh."

I wouldn't even get bus fare home.

Don't kid yourself. At work, sweating the small stuff (to borrow from the Ford Motor Company) is *Job One*. In fact, it's your ass if you don't sweat it. This is, after all, the job you depend on for your food and shelter! So, you better damn well sweat the small stuff. You better damn well feel a little anxious and under pressure if your work isn't done with competence, on time, and within the budget. Sweating the small stuff is being accountable. Sweating the small stuff is understanding the importance, and yes, occasional DRAMA, of deadlines. Sweating the small stuff from your "demanding boss" should be a major priority for you. He or she is the person who judges your continued employment, for God's sake! He or she is what stands between you and your next raise, your new house, and your health insurance. Those are big things you most certainly should sweat.

The sad news is that apparently a lot of people have taken Dr. Carlson's book seriously. Like my friend, Sam. Sam told me he wanted a job where he could finally relax and not sweat the small stuff so much. So, he went to work for an athletic shoe manufacturer whose mission was to provide, "the greatest working environment ever." The company let the employees design their own flexible hours. They had job sharing and job trading so employees wouldn't be bored. Young mothers could bring their babies to work and receive free daycare. All of the walls were painted in carefully researched colors that allegedly produced a calming effect. The company built a fully furnished gym, offered free personal trainers and free lunchroom treats. They didn't even believe in putting quota pressure on the sales force. They believed in, "letting the product sell itself." Employees got bonuses for coming to work on time. Oh, and did I mention every employee got free shoes? It was a very cool (and extremely low stress) place to work.

That is, until the president dropped the bomb that the company was in serious cash flow trouble and that everyone was going to have to pull together to save the company. (Translation: cut expenses and salaries)

What was my friend's reaction? Did his loyalty and honor bubble to the surface to help rescue the company that offered him such a generous and peaceful environment? Hell no! He felt betrayed. His dream job was reneging on its published mission statement. Now, he was being asked to work like a normal person. The mood around the company wasn't unity. It was mutiny.

People didn't pull together. They pulled out. The copy machines hummed, 'round the clock, churning out updated resumes.

Maybe the president should have sweated some of the small stuff...like productivity, revenue, and expenses; instead of hiring freeloaders like my friend.

The company eventually filed for Chapter 11 bankruptcy protection. As you could probably predict, my friend was livid over his non-existent severance package.

Of course, the utopian work place does exist. But you won't believe where I found it. In the unlikely desert town of Laughlin, Nevada.

I produced a human resource training film for a tiny retail store called *The Watch Man*. *The Watch Man* may be small but they sell an astounding 20,000 wrist watches a year. I've never seen such giddy employees. The owners offer them free bowling nights and in-house cooking contests. Each week, a different employee's picture is featured in their newspaper ads; along with the store's weekly "specials." The entire staff even gathers to sing during the morning sales meeting. Wow! What gives?

How do they make it work?

The Watch Man's mission statement is two-tiered. They want Lifetime Customers and Lifetime Employees. First and foremost, the employees never lose sight of the fact that they are in the business of selling watches. If they sell enough watches, the fun continues. If not, changes have to be made. So, they make sure that every customer gets what they want. They give away fresh batteries to anybody who wants one. They offer a lifetime warranty; even on a $19 dollar watch. Plus, they treat every person who walks in the door like the richest person on earth. *The Watch Man* employees indeed sweat ALL of the small stuff.

Start sweating today or die a painful, unemployed death.

IT'S ALWAYS ABOUT YOU:

Are you really sweating the small stuff or is the small stuff what you were hired to do? Do you find yourself complaining about doing work that is beneath you? Or, as a manager, are you frustrated that work isn't getting done because you aren't demanding performance standards? How do you feel about deadlines? Do you finish ahead of time or do you always turn your work in late? Encourage yourself and others to sweat the small stuff. Details are vitally important because details matter to your customers and to your clients. Caring about the details and sweating the small stuff is what will make you successful; while your competition worries about painting the office walls in psychologically soothing colors.

CHAPTER 5

THOSE "CHICKEN SOUP" BOOKS ARE FOR FOOLS.

I know this is supposed to be a book about YOU and YOUR work life, but you'll see the connection in a moment.

Comedian Mort Sahl told me a joke about the invaluable healing powers of steaming poultry broth. "There is a poor Jewish farmer who only had two chickens. When one of his chickens got sick, the farmer killed the other one to make soup."

Unfortunately, these books don't have the same effect. They are nothing more than bathroom pulp targeted at every available book-buying segment of our population. And we are foolish enough to keep buying them!

About a year ago, I was in a Barnes and Noble and joked to my wife that, "If these Chicken Soup books really wanted to be unique, there would be a "Chicken Soup for the Death Row

Inmate's Soul." I was shocked when the clerk (who overheard me) showed me one called, *Chicken Soup for the Prisoner's Soul.* What?! Uplifting stories to provide laughter, insight and inspiration for the con in lock up? I love prison movies and I faithfully watch OZ on HBO but I swear it wouldn't be nearly as cool and gritty if cons were weeping over that book.

So what's my real beef? Am I jealous? Nope. They are much too sappy for me to want a piece.

I just wish they wouldn't pretend to inspire spiritual healing when the primary magic of these books is their brilliant capitalistic engine. And I say that with genuine respect and affection for their author; Jack Canfield.

I think Jack is a marketing marvel to be able to transform these "stories" into an entire industry. He must have laughed himself nuts when his simple idea of compiling tales took off and became a phenomenon. And since you can never predict a phenomenon, here's why I think it happened. My guess is that, as a nation, we are so beaten up and beaten down by this life, that we're hungry for any morsel of good news. Jack just gave it to us in easy-to-digest hunks. He found the "better mousetrap" we've all heard about that makes people rich. Wow, did it make him rich!

Today, there are Chicken Soup books for the Mother's Souls, the Expectant Mothers Soul, the Fathers Soul, the Kids Soul, the Little Soul (a book for humans younger than kids?) the Pre-Teen Soul, the Teenagers Soul, the Teenagers Soul with tough problems, the Parents Soul, the Couples Soul, the Singles Soul (we can't forget the people who aren't in relationships and don't have children) the Grandparents Soul, the Golden Soul (over 60 years old), the (war) Veterans Soul, and even the Surviving Soul. Jack has successfully covered every possible age group who might need to "open the heart and rekindle the spirit" of their lives.

But then, he expanded the series to include The Travelers Soul? Are travelers in a different biological group than those already listed? No! Sure, we travel. But our problems are the same as before we left on our journey.

Then came the sports editions like the Golfers Soul, the Sports Fans Soul, and the Baseball Fans Soul; obviously, the largest sport book buying population segment. But I noticed there wasn't a book for the Ice Dancing Soul. Why not? Because there aren't enough people in the sport to warrant a printing?

That wasn't enough.

The top religions got their books, too. There is *a Chicken Soup for the Christian Soul*. Now, you, Jack Canfield, and me know that there are a ton of Christians worldwide. So many that the *Chicken Soup for the Christian Family Soul* soon followed. Christians must love to read separately because there is also the Christian *Woman's* Soul book. Yes, the Jews got their *Chicken Soup for the Jewish Soul*, too. But the Buddhist Soul has so far been patently ignored. Maybe it's because they are already at peace. Or, because they don't go to enough book signings? You need lots of bodies to make a book a best seller. Want bodies, Jack? Try publishing a Chicken Soup the Illegal Alien's Soul.

Can't you just hear Jack's mind whirring? "Hmm, what other giant population segment with disposable income have we missed?" Not many. *Chicken Soup for the Cat and Dog Lovers Soul* seems to sell pretty well. So does the one for the Gardener's Soul.

And even the one for the Veggies Souls. But *Chicken Soup for the Writer's Soul?* That's on your book sellers shelf. But why? Oh, I get it. It is either because (1) Writers are tormented (mostly by themselves) (2) Almost everyone thinks they have a book inside them waiting to get out...or (3) Writers and would-be writers visit lots of bookstores to buy books about writing/writers.

Very clever, Jack.

With all of these "comfort food" story books there is yet one more that I see with tiresome regularity. In fact, I can't tell you how many awards banquets I've M.C'd where someone got a *Chicken Soup for The Soul at Work; 101 stories of Courage, Compassion, and Creativity in the workplace.* Yes, even employers think someone needs a break from their job enough to recharge their soul with courage, compassion and creativity. Nice sentiment from the boss, huh? Thumbing through one, while eating my award banquet Chicken Cordon-Dry, I thought to myself, "I don't know if this helps people but it sure is long & boring." So, I read few reviews to see if I was missing something. This was an actual reader review posted on Amazon.Com (April 2002).

> *"The stories all appeared long-winded (actually, verbose), boring, and non-inspiring. Although the other books are all wonderful to read and reread over and over again, containing countless inspirational stories, these weren't even worth wading through the first time. I hate to say it, but this one seems to have been written solely to make a buck,*

padding out the most boring experiences to compile a book. They aren't inspirational and aren't interesting."

Oops. Jack. Did you and your team get caught making a buck with weak material?

Don't get mad at him or his army of Chicken Soupers. The music industry suckers us like this all the time. How many times have you loved a band's first album, ran out to buy the second album, and it stinks? No surprise. The band worked for years to get the material ready for the first album. It was a huge hit and now the record label wants albums #2 and #3 by the end of the year. But it's hard to demand inspiration...upon demand.

Alright, so the books cover all bases. So what if they run out of steam in a few market segments. No harm done, right?

Wrong.

Here's my issue with these mega-sellers; the systemic problem that convinces me that these books are for us "fools." The effects of these stories don't last! These wonderful stories of courage, inspiration, and compassion don't affect real behavioral change. Test your own family like I tested mine.

Last Christmas, our family opened our presents and several people got Chicken Soup for the...whatever, as gifts. They laughed and even wept as they read stories about people just like them who had bigger problems. I repeatedly heard, "Jeez, I guess I shouldn't complain about my in laws, my weight, my bald spot, my combination skin, my grumpy boss, my evaporating 401K, my (insert your personal dilemma here). Light bulbs of understanding brilliantly burst on...and just as suddenly, switched off.

By the end of the third turkey sandwich, my family was back arguing with each other over the same tired disputes, complaining about their weight, their fleeting hairlines, combination skin and...well, you get the picture.

So if you're a boss, think twice before giving these books as business gifts. Because, an employee will think you MEAN what you're implying by giving it; that you actually care about them. And we both know that they can Chicken Soup themselves all they want. But if their department or unit or region isn't making more money than it costs to run it, their little chicken soup booty is going to be reading, *Chicken Soup for the Unemployed Soul.*

IT'S ALWAYS ABOUT YOU:

I'll bet your life is tough. Your work is hard. Your hours are long. And unfair circumstances bump you around; every single day. But you know what? So does everybody else. Stand tough and laugh at the bruises life leaves you; knowing that you can get 6-8 hours rest, wake up tomorrow; and be ready for some more. Be resilient. The issues may change, but you are always going to be in a constant state of hurt and healing. Sadly, no Chicken Soup book is going to prevent that. If that notion upsets you, read *Chicken Soup for the Prisoner's Soul.*

You'll shut up and feel blessed.

CHAPTER 6

10 STUPID THINGS DR. LAURA SAYS TO GET YOU TO BUY HER BOOKS.

What does Dr. Laura have to do with YOUR Career?

More than enough to scare you.

In fact, the whole acceptance of the psychotherapy-victimnation culture has invaded the workplace. Many companies now offer psychotherapy as a reimbursed insurance item. So, if you haven't seen a therapist yet, odds are that you'll soon get the thrill of shelling out cash to expose your life to a total stranger.

Bringing us back to Dr. Laura Schlessinger.

She has a lot to say about people in corporate America because she has "treated" so many top corporate executives;

maybe even *your* boss. Without naming names, Laura told me that many of the high level executives she has treated didn't think they deserved to be in charge. They lived in fear that, any day now, they would be "found out" and canned. Interesting, isn't it? She says it's because many successful people feel guilty for their success. They have low self-esteem and honestly don't think they are qualified to be making such big decisions or drawing big pay. (Are you nodding your head in agreement?)

I came to know Dr. Laura because she was my marriage counselor. I saw her every week for almost a year; right up to the divorce. But that was long before she was a world famous radio psychologist. Long before she was a best selling author. And waaay before I stopped believing that pop psychologists could solve our problems.

My experience with Dr. Laura was different than what you may have heard on the radio. I liked her. She was smart and insightful. And, in my case, she never berated me. I was paying and she was listening.

Why did Dr. Laura become the most popular woman on the radio? Because whether you like her or not, she is bold enough to stand for something. She has an uncompromising view of morality; mixed with an annoying smugness. Nonetheless, it was a "hook" that Americans could sink their collective "issues" into. She is heard on more than 500 radio stations; which translates to something near 20 million listeners. In broadcasting, that's monster status. Dr. Laura has a long term radio contract rumored to be worth more than 90 million dollars. Her rabid fans preface their calls with the Dr. Laura chant, "I'm my kid's Mom."

Unfortunately, they think if they suck up to Laura, she will cut them some slack when they reveal their "unique dilemma."

It doesn't work.

Most of the time, Laura quickly locks horns, chastises them, and dismisses her minions within seconds; often pausing afterward to reflect on their abject stupidity. (Incidentally, I do, too) What I find amazing is that after dispensing such radio wrath, she can turn on a dime and sweetly hawk her books, T-shirts, coffee mugs, monthly newsletter, and even better rates on life insurance; all of which I'm sure make her a second fortune. She is a rare cocktail of the nouveau liberal fascist capitalist.

I have no problem with that.

It's the best selling books that scorch my toast. I'm talking about Dr. Laura's empire of the, *10 Things People do that are Stupid* books. Not that I blame her for cashing in. I don't. If you have the exposure, make some hay. But I DO blame the imbeciles who buy the books. And for living up to their stupidity. Do they buy the books to highlight the reasons they're screwed up? Or, so they can show the book to their mate and validate the blame? Surely, they can't be buying them to glean actual insight? Because they call Laura's show, admit they bought the book and still defend their bad judgement.

Whatever the reasons, Laura fuels the fire and has spun off, *10 Things that Women Do to Mess Up Their Lives* to a men's version, a parent's version, a family version, and a couples version. In every case, the list is confined to tidy ten reasons. If you haven't read the original book, here is a primer that will barely do it justice. You are Stupid if you get too attached, fall blindly in love, move in together too soon, let passion override reality, expect too much (or too little), let abuse reign, act like a victim, have babies out of wedlock, forgive a cheater, lie, steal, or kill.

If you can't find your pedestrian problem on that list, then you can buy her, *"10 Commandments"* book. It covers the rest. In fact, the only way your particular dilemma can't be found among this collection is if you're a single cell organism waiting to evolve into a book buyer.

Either way, you can't escape.

It was Dr. Laura's success that made me realize what a deliciously accepted scam "pop psychology" has become in the past twenty-five years. It surely wasn't popular in the Shafer household. Growing up in the rugged timberlands of the Pacific Northwest, we were told that only crazy people went to brain doctors. And even if you went, you never told anyone. It brought shame on the family. A stigma only forgiven if you tithed generously to the Presbyterian church.

But now as an enlightened adult (I never said the word enlightened until therapy), I certainly get the appeal. I went for the same reason many others go. I wanted to know why my marriage fell apart. I was hurting and wanted a quick fix.

The amazing windfall for the shrinks is that their patients want that quick fix when they are in a hopelessly irrational state of mind. That means money is no object. We buy books, tapes, CD's, get hypnotized, and happily spill our guts to total strangers for $150 an hour. So desperate are some of us, that if we can't get an appointment when we need it, we will pick up the cordless phone and call a radio shrink like Dr. Laura, Dr. Tony Grant, Dr. Joy Brown, Dr. Barbara DeAngeles, or you name your local favorite.

And her callers expect instant miracles!

Listen to Dr. Laura's callers and you will hear that they demand instant, immaculate therapy. An out-of-breath-from-crying housewife will relate what sounds like a family-shattering problem and astoundingly expect Laura to resolve the issue in less than thirty "radio" seconds.

Golly! Laura is right. Most people really *are* stupid.

These folks need to get a grip. There is no quick fix. Even if you do spend an hour a week "on the couch," you are still on your own to figure out what went wrong; and hopefully not repeat it. Time and distance seems to be the only thing that really works.

I learned another lesson about psychologists from my oldest son, Adam. He was being a rebellious 9th grader when he and some buddies were arrested for breaking into their Junior High School janitorial closet. They stole some Windex and toilet paper. (I kept hoping he did it because he didn't know where the spare rolls were kept) His mother insisted that we see a counselor and I reluctantly agreed. We sat on a bad plaid couch talking to the nice therapist who said, "Adam, we need you to understand that you have broken a contract with your parents. So, we are going to write up a new contract that states that you are to come home right after school. And secondly, that you won't see your best friend (co-criminal) for a few weeks. And..." At that point Adam broke in and said, "I'm not signing any god damned contract." The nice man said, "I hear you. But your parents made a contract to keep a roof over your head. Do you understand we all have contractual obligations to keep?" Adam wasn't going for this "contract" nonsense. "I don't have to sign contracts to live there," he snorted.

I'd had enough. I stood up and announced, "The appointment is over. There won't be any contracts but there will be some rules. First rule is, I am going to go home and take all of the wheels off of your car. (He had a VW Bug he was fixing up to drive when he turned 16) If you obey the rules, I'll put one wheel back on each week." Adam understood *that* unwritten contract and we didn't have any problems after that. That's my new formula for raising kids, they don't need therapy. They need love, direction, accountability and consequences.

What about the truly screwed up and tormented artist types?

Being in show business, I regularly hear people talking about their "head docs" and how much they are learning "in therapy" or "in group." It's a joke. My proof that therapy "junkies" don't use the advice of their "experts" stems from my observation that they never seem to get "cured." My friends have the same problems today that they've had for years. But, they love going back to their brain bender for even more elusive insight into their self absorbed lives. Let me recant. That's not entirely correct. Lately, some go as an excuse to renew their Prozac prescriptions.

I always thought a good business would be a chain of Drive-Thru Psychologists. You know, Marital Spats $50 bucks. Mother/Daughter Issues $75. Or, you could Super-Size-It and bring in your whole family. Too absurd? Then why do so many people call their friends in the middle of the night to get the number of their astrologer, palm reader, psychic, shakra or aura analysts?

Save your time and money.

Just take the wheels off your car.

IT'S ALWAYS ABOUT YOU:

Are you in therapy? Why do you go? What answers are you looking for that your friends and family haven't been telling you for years? What answers are you afraid to face up to? She/he isn't coming back? You are not going to be rehired? Do you roll over and die or do you live another day? Or are you going to finally wrestle with a childhood trauma? We all go through painful times. But there is no quick fix. Time and distance from the pain is all that really works. Understand that life is an ongoing series of U-turns, Roadblocks and Dead Ends. We all have to adjust to the unexpected. And by the way, so did our parents. They did the best they were capable of doing, at the time. So stop being mad at, and blaming anyone else for your problems. If someone has inadvertently hurt you, practice a little forgiveness. Whatever your problem, you don't need to buy a "10 Things You did that was Stupid book" unless you need verification that you are truly stupid. Or, try this profound angle. If you made a mistake, fix it on your own. Make a call. Write a letter. Arrange a face to face chat. Don't die without making things right in your life. It will eat you up inside if you don't. You know what feels good and what feels bad. Stop doing things that make you feel bad. Start doing more of the things that make you feel good. In the meantime, exercise common sense and willpower. Realize that you don't need a guru to orchestrate your life. Stop thinking that another person, who doesn't know you, can make the best decisions for You.

Thank you.

Now, pull ahead and pay at the second window.

CHAPTER 7

THE ONE-MINUTE MANAGER GOT LAID OFF.

Ken Blanchard's runaway best seller was required reading for all of us college management/marketing students. It even made good sense when it was published 20 years ago. But it's terribly stale and irrelevant today.

Oh, the principles of reducing stress, giving one-minute reprimands and one minute praises definitely eased up on the stress of yesterday's managers. But it doesn't work anymore. The One-Minute Managers have been laid off. Who is left to "manage for a minute?" Nobody. Hence, delegation is dead. And the people on the firing line aren't good enough to trust with enough responsibility to become One-Minute Managers who can delegate. They can't even accomplish basic chores. Companies are so busy divesting, merging and acquiring that the same employee could do three totally different jobs in the same year. Often times, managers disappear and never return.

At a conference in Palm Beach, Florida, I spoke to Marcus Buckingham (author of, *First, Break All the Rules*). Marcus has done extensive Gallop Poll research to authenticate that only 30% of the workforce in any organization is actively engaged in trying to do a good job. The rest are marking time or worse; actively undermining the organization's success.

Why? Because (1) They have experienced incredible emotional upheaval from being scared about being replaced, let go, or fired and (2) They don't have clear roles or job descriptions to keep them interested in being productive. So much for increased productivity through merger and acquisition.

One of my businesses is writing and producing funny Human Resource training films. You can't imagine how elementary the scripts have to be. We actually have to instruct people to SMILE at the customer! How can you delegate real responsibility to a person who doesn't even know when to smile?

More importantly, how did this breakdown happen in the first place?

First, I blame us parents. I really do. Baby boomer parents haven't taught their children to be responsible, accountable and resourceful when faced with new and challenging responsibilities. (I certainly count my own parenting blunders in this group) So when these people are promoted too soon, have no experience, or can't do the job, they either collapse from the pressure or assign the job to someone else.

Often, it lands in the lap of someone far less qualified than themselves.

Secondly, I blame the technology revolution that has made mergers so cost effective. A chain of banks can merge with another chain of banks, network their computers, eliminate half of the employees, and collect a service fee when you visit the branch. Isn't that unbelievable? They have the nerve to charge a fee if you want to talk to any of the remaining staff!? Maybe that's why the banks encourage you to use the ATM? Because they know the people left behind can't possibly answer your questions.

I see this in the TV business all the time. A reasonably capable "assistant" gets promoted to "manager" because the previous manager left for a better job with a rival company. The assistant-promoted-to-manager doesn't really have enough experience to do the job but is the least worst candidate. Soon, the New Manager is overwhelmed. So, the New Manager hires an assistant. Eventually, the two of them find themselves in a position to make important decisions. But they are too afraid to do anything because they might screw up and lose their jobs.

Instead, they stall. They commission "studies." They order focus groups. They assign task forces...and so on. They'll try anything to justify saying, "NO" so that risky decisions can be avoided. Screech! Progress grinds to a halt. Innovation and creativity are stuck in the corporate mud. The irony of this is that the new manager will probably get a glowing personal appraisal for zero errors; which sets him/her up for another promotion!

It makes a sane person want to scream!

When did fear become more popular than competence? Some of my greatest successes have come from tackling (and taking responsibility for) projects I didn't know anything about. (See the "Back Up Your Lies With the Truth" Chapter)

I never minded jumping into jobs without experience because I knew I could quickly learn them. I figured if a human invented it, I was human enough to execute it. I was only a "C" student but by the time it came to actually DO the job, I was trained and ready. I also noticed that most people were afraid to commit. So, in an environment of fear, I was a bit of a maverick. Since I already thought of myself as fired, what did I have to lose? I didn't know it at the time but I was faking leadership! That attitude may have seemed arrogant but it also made me fearless. I got a lot of great new experiences as a result.

Another "conventional wisdom" business model that champions delegation over practicality is the notion that we shouldn't MICROMANAGE people. The idea is something like, "don't get too involved with your team. Even if you have more experience, let them succeed or fail on their own."

That's just crazy!

Will somebody PLEASE do us all a favor and micromanage something?! Anything!?

So many of the companies I've worked for are management top heavy; brimming with executive assistants, assistant managers, managers, middle managers, regional managers, and national managers. Nobody seems to be doing any of the grunt work, anymore. Consequently, their customers spend time filling the complaint boxes with letters. Can't somebody PLEASE micromanage just long enough until the work gets done right? Or, at least teach people what you know before you go on vacation.

The extinction of the One-Minute Manager, in my irritated opinion, pinpoints why most customer service is so rotten. Nobody is low enough on the Totem Pole to actually care about us; the client or customer.

Recently, my wife called *The Singing Store* in Sherman Oaks, California to see if they had a particular CD she wanted. The clerk said, "We are very busy and I can't talk to you now." My wife said, "Could you call me back when you aren't so busy?" The clerk actually said, "I can't because we're going to be busy all day." Why would a clerk say something so stupid? Because the "boss" got lazy and delegated the company's lifeblood to a dolt, that's why.

We all witnessed the most widespread example of bad delegation in the virtually extinct DotCom world. The Dot Com start-ups imploded for that very reason. These young lions of management had everyone fooled; for a while. They were Harvard/Stanford caliber graduates who dazzled us by writing "scalable business models" and organizing "strategic alliances" but they didn't know one wit about managing people, systems, or even keeping enough cash in a checking account. They delegated all the duties downward until nobody with any skill was left to keep them in business. You know, skills like selling and inventory control and delivery systems. The basics. Those of us who were mesmerized into investing with these 21st Century snake oil salesmen forgot that these "geniuses" had never managed anything outside of the classroom. Shame on us, too.

And do you recall how they kept telling us that profit wasn't important? It was all about "valuation." Well apparently, valuation has the life expectancy of helium because valuation sure as hell couldn't keep the dot.com balloon in the air. When the E-world crashed, it took the economy and a lot of people's life savings with it.

As I reread that I sounded a bit like a bitter man who lost a ton of money with the dot.com stocks. Oops, busted.

See, I remember, that when I was in the pet business, I didn't have an eager parade of speculating investors. It was MY OWN cash on the line. I couldn't buy more parakeets until we sold the ones we had. Sales projections had to be very tight to the actual sales figures or we'd be trapping our own rats for snake food!

IT'S ALWAYS ABOUT YOU:

What makes you think you can manage in a minute? Is your management structure that deep that you have somebody to manage? Or are you IT? Before you delegate and decide you can manage your department in a minute, make sure the job will get done if you're gone; done just the way you would do it. If you are the only one doing that job, wait until you can train your replacement. Get your part right and you'll build a strong foundation for your company and an even firmer foundation for your career. Got it? Good. Take the day off.

YOUR JOB

IS

TERMINAL...

&

OTHER

GOOD NEWS.

CHAPTER 8

YOUR JOB

IS TERMINAL.

One of the best reasons to stay self-absorbed is to realize that your job will be eliminated. Or, at the very least, your job will change dramatically...or be folded into a merger in ways you cannot imagine, today. Sorry to break the news to you but I can see it from here.

Impossible? How can that be when your company has been around since the last century? Ask the folks at Enron, Hewlett Packard, A,T & T, Consolidated Freightways, United Airlines, and WorldCom if *they* saw it coming.

Sadly, I have seen this happen over and over again because I get hired to come in and boost morale after the big "down sizing." Excuse me, "right-sizing" is the politically correct surgical strike term, these days.

Check this out. I was the guest speaker for a major banking chain's annual Christmas party. I mean this was the most respected of financial institutions. The been-around-forever kind. Their dapper President stood before a group of five hundred shaky top management people to tell them the rumors of an impending sale were absolutely false and that nobody in the room had to worry about losing his/her job.

Fast forward six months: I was hired by the conglomerate that gobbled them up! This time the sophomore meeting planner said, "Ross, our people have been put through the ringer, and we heard you're good at getting people to laugh at themselves?" Gulp.

I really don't think the former bank president was lying. I just don't think he knew what his board was cooking up behind his well groomed back.

Things go wrong. Plans get derailed. And yes, YOU can be replaced; regardless of how well you have mapped out your career strategy. So, what do you do? Live in constant terror? NO! The solution is to expect roadblocks and detours. Expect that a bigger fish may devour your company. Go to work expecting that one of your team members is going to majorly mess up and affect your job security. I'm not talking about adopting an attitude of negativity and paranoia. Just be realistic and don't get caught with your resume down. Too many factors are out of your control, right? And it's the out-of-your-control elements that will drive you bats...unless you're ready for them!

Better yet, make yourself "fire proof." Develop skills that your company absolutely needs. And make sure these are skills that are also transferable to other companies and organizations. Keep yourself in a constant state-of-YOUR-art. You'll be undeniably invaluable in the next position. Stay fully trained. Be ready to hit the ground running; able to instantly make money for your next employer.

How simple is that?

How can you possibly be unemployed if you are the best at what you do? Personal productivity and your ability to recognize that you are a cog in the profit center wheel is gold to any employer. Know that. Live that. And believe that anybody would be thrilled...no...proud to have YOU on their team. Wow. I got myself so worked up I almost forgot to give you a good example of what I'm talking about.

I learned about the temporary nature of my business, television, from "America's Teenager," Dick Clark.

I met Dick on his *TV's Bloopers and Practical Jokes* show in 1985. I had made some TV Goofs on our local TV show and I wound up on his show in some funny, yet embarrassing clips.

One day, Dick asked me to fly to Los Angeles and be a guest on "Bloopers" and talk about the *Louie, Louie* phenomenon we had started in Washington. (More on this later) After the taping he said, "I have a feeling you could go places in this business. But remember this. Your job is terminal. Television is terminal. Every job you have in this business will eventually go away."

Pretty hard to swallow; especially considering the time I was investing in trying to "make it."

But he was Dick Clark, for God's sake. He must know something.

I asked him how *he* handled being "cancelled?" He told me he didn't worry about it. "I have had more cancelled TV shows than anyone else in this business and you know why? Because

I've had more TV shows on the air than anyone else in this business. In fact, I am looking forward to my next ten cancellations."

What a great way to look at failure. Which isn't failure, at all. It's just working your way towards your next victory.

I have a friend who is a research scientist and says he doesn't mind performing a thousand experiments that fail because he gets giddy thinking he is getting that much closer to being right.

Getting bounced from your job can even happen in the most tenured of occupations.

My friend, Doug, has been in the teaching profession for over twenty years. It's been a stable career for a guy who is always at the top of his evaluation reviews. If anybody was safe and secure it was Doug.

Until this past year.

His school district announced that his school would have to shave their budget by a million bucks. That meant that no new teachers would be hired. And, *his* job as school counselor would be eliminated. (You've probably seen the same thing happen with school music teachers around the country). Mind you, Doug wasn't entirely out of work. The district would have placed him elsewhere but not in the kind of job he was accustomed to loving. Or the extra helpings of Chipped Beef Surprise on alternate Thursdays. So, Doug and his family had to sell their home and move 300 miles away to find a similar job.

Still think the odds are in your favor that YOUR job is safe? If you do, Las Vegas gives away free hotel rooms to people like you.

IT'S ALWAYS ABOUT YOU:

What would you do if you came to work one day and found out they didn't need your position anymore? Do you have a back up plan? You are always going to be your own best job security as long as you consider yourself already fired. Always be ready to put your Plan "B" into action. I love Plan "B". Instead of panicking when your first plan (job) goes south, you already have another one ready to take its place. Do that and you won't freak out and make bad decisions under pressure. You'll just slip into your alternative mode. The back up plan will also make you the envy of your office. People will automatically follow your "natural born leadership skills." See how easy it is to fool people? I admire people who update their resumes every two months - even when they are very happy in their current jobs. So, unless you own the copyright to the song, "Happy Birthday," or you are a tenured professor who has never slept with a willing student, there is no such thing as job security.

CHAPTER 9

GOAL SETTING IS STUPID.

Comedian George Miller, has said this about goals. "My girlfriend is always harping on me about my goals. Do I have any goals? What are my goals? I told her, Yes, I have goals. I want to have sex with you and then leave!" I don't know how rarely George achieves that goal but he is both funny and hilariously specific.

Setting goals doesn't work. I've been at corporate retreats where companies roll out the annual sales goals only to watch the employees faint from apoplexy. Goals are pure fantasy unless you have a specific plan to achieve them. And of course, nothing unexpected and weird gets in the way. Like a war or a tornado that levels your plant. Simply announcing or wishing sales to be higher doesn't make it so. Worse, it may have the reverse effect if the team thinks the goal is unrealistic.

I bet you've personally devoted months, maybe years of thought to YOUR career "goals," your income projections, your one-year, your five-year, and maybe even your retirement goals. Maybe you have even written them down or stuck them under a photo magnet on your fridge. Sad to say, but without a disciplined roadmap, those goals are worthless. You know why? Because writing down goals doesn't mean a thing until you realize that the goal is only the destination. How much thought have you given to the journey? Your answer should be "lots." You'll need to fill in a lot of holes between where you are now and where you want to go. A lot of work, huh? Well, each step has to be mapped out if you want to be able to check your position and stay on the right path. Mapping also shows you how far you are from your goal and what route to take next.

That's exactly how writers work. They plot the course; step by tedious step. Novelists can't sit down and write 500 pages front to back. They outline. They put ideas on 3X5 cards and pin them all over the wall. Then, they move the cards around until the story makes sense. Usually, they sit down and write one chapter at a time; using cause and effect to make it intelligible. After a while, their collection of individual chapters equals one novel.

The deep voiced singer, Lou Rawls, taught me a lot about "stacking" my nightclub act to accomplish goals with the audience. He takes great pains in devising his song list before each performance. Each song is "stacked" in a specific order to segue smoothly into the next one. That way he can dictate the mood and emotion he wants the crowd to experience. By the end of the evening, each member of the audience feels invested in Lou and his music.

As a comedian, if my goal is to get a standing ovation, I have to carefully build each joke "hunk" to take the listener on a predetermined funny journey. The first five minutes are designed to introduce myself and give the audience a reason to stay invested in me for an hour. Then, I try a few comic premises and let the audience determine the subjects that interest them. In the final two minutes, I stack the jokes so that the laughs come every five seconds. Then, if I end with my very strongest joke or story; I'll get my biggest, longest laugh. If I have done my job correctly I'll build my act to end "on a roll." My success gauge is if the audience responds with 25 seconds of exit applause or if they come to their feet. It may sound like manipulation but the audience gets what they want and I accomplish my goal.

So the next time your boss gives you a goal, ask him/her how you all plan to get there. You can't just voodoo an increase of sales by 15%. There has to be a well thought out strategy. Strategy gives you confidence, direction, a measuring device, and usually includes a Plan "B." If he or she can't do that, then make it your goal to find another job.

IT'S ALWAYS ABOUT YOU:

What goals have you written down? Where are they now? Can you be more specific about the steps in between now and your ultimate goal? If so, fill in the blanks and start doing things to check off your list. Make a Plan "B" and a Plan "C." You may never need them but it's nice to have them on hand in an emergency or if things take a turn you didn't expect. Periodically check your list, see where you are, and try not to get distracted. Oh, and if your plan isn't working, your plan may be flawed. Switch gears and try something else. (See Chapter #27)

Finally, don't let fear keep you from charging ahead.

Regret is far more traumatizing than the fear.

CHAPTER 10

FIND YOUR

BREAKING POINT.

We all have breaking points. The sooner you find yours, the sooner you'll stop wasting your time on a dead end career and start using your time and talents toward something you enjoy.

My breaking point changed the course of my life in every possible way.

After college, I wanted to be an entrepreneur. I fell in love with the idea of being my own boss. Who wouldn't? Naturally, everyone I loved and respected said I was nuts. "Ross, you have a degree. Get a job and use it."

I was determined to prove them all wrong.

So I took my life savings (about $9,000) and before long...became the miserable co-owner of a stereo shop on the verge of bankruptcy.

My partner, Bill Jones, and I desperately needed a Plan "B." One twelve pack of Budweiser later, we landed on the brainstorm to mix a stereo store with a pet shop. Hmm, pets aren't seasonal, we thought. And we figured what better "draw" than cute little puppies and kittens? We could anchor them in the rear of the store so that our customers would have to walk by the stereo gear on the way to see the critters. The same basic strategy grocery stores use to trick you with milk and eggs. The promotional hook of, "America's ONLY Stereo and Pet Shop" was certain to make us one of the nation's most popular roadside attractions.

We weren't wrong.

The advertising campaigns wrote themselves. "Come to us for all your woofers and tweeters." Gimmicks like our "Pet Fashion Show" and "Hamster Drag Races" drove tons of traffic through our door. Unfortunately, they came to look at the animals and buy Monkey Chow; not to purchase speakers. Consequently, the pet store got bigger while the listening rooms grew silent. Not our master plan but you go with what sells, right?

Look, I love pets as much as you do. But, standing daily guard over a store full of barking, whining, and scratching creatures turned a guy like me into a whack job. The dung maintenance alone extinguished my spirit to live. And, pets are disturbing on another level. Cuddly lower food chain animals tend to EAT each other. That's right. Eat, as in chew and swallow.

We had a talking parrot who pecked our one legged Cockatiel to death during a Labor Day sale.

We had an eight-foot boa constrictor that slithered out of his cage and into the aviary where he devoured seven parakeets -

in full view of our customers. I took three of us grown men to wrestle him out of the window!

Oh, and there was the time I invited a local third grade class to watch baby hamsters being born. The kids gathered at the big display case as the chubby, fuzzy Mommy hamster waddled right up the glass cage and popped out six bald babies; right on cue. Giggles. Oooohs. Awwws.

Then, the Daddy hamster came over and ATE the newborns! Screams. Crying. Customers evacuating.

This called for fast thinking. I tried to convince the kids that the Daddy hamster washes the babies after they are born and that he will spit them out later when they are clean. I may go to hell for that lie.

It didn't take us long to realize it was nearly impossible to make a profit when your inventory is in a constant state of Natural Selection. My pride of being a young entrepreneur was muddied by the reality of working more than 70 hours a week for a take-home of less than $200 hundred bucks. I'd really screwed up my big plan.

Ironically, the day before Mt. St. Helens blew, I myself erupted. For 30 minutes, I tried to "net" a specific spotted Goldfish for a regular (and quite finicky) customer. Not an easy task when you consider this two-inch freckled carp was in a tank with at least 500 pals. I attempted dip after dip. But, each time I raised the net, the customer insisted I had snagged the wrong one.

I finally snapped. My breaking point lit up like Vegas on New Years Eve.

I grabbed what I remember to be something the size of a Tuna net and drug it through the entire tank - scooping up at least 60 goldfish. Then, I shouted at the elderly man, "Trust me. The one you want is in there! The rest are on me!"

Man, what had I done with my life? I hated going to work and I was getting seriously depressed. All day long, I would watch the clock tick by until it struck 9pm. Then, I would lock the door on another day and stumble home for one more microwaved meal. I prayed for Sunday (my day off) where I would hook up with friends and wash down too much pizza with way too much beer. I was pegging the dial on the bathroom scale and I hid my identity behind a shaggy beard and shoulder length hair. (The bloated evidence is on the back cover of this book.)

The highlight of my weeknights was collapsing into my garage-sale-Lazy Boy recliner to watch Johnny Carson on *The Tonight Show*. I'd forget my day, marvel at the celebrities he'd interview, and howl when he did impressions in funny costumes. In my mind, Johnny Carson had the coolest job in the world. That was it. I only had one choice. I needed to quit this mess and go after Johnny's job.

It took me six years but I wound up competing head-to-head against Johnny Carson as the late night host on the Fox Network's *Late Show*. Johnny wrote me a nice note when Rupert Murdoch (who owned the Fox) was rattling swords to buy NBC. The note was to the effect of, "If Rupert buys NBC, I'll see you at the Christmas Party."

I would never have read that note if I hadn't found my breaking point. (Although, I might have eventually shaved.)

IT'S ALWAYS ABOUT YOU:

Have you found your own breaking point, yet? Don't worry if you haven't. It will be obvious and significant. You will absolutely know when it's time to change your direction. A big sign is when you hate getting up in the morning. Your stomach will ache. You will think of excuses to call in sick. You will think that your life means nothing and you will wonder why you were put on earth. Then, you will find yourself updating your resume or asking around about other jobs. What would make you the happiest? What is your passion? Can you make money at it? Can you be involved in a peripheral way that exposes you to the fun and still takes advantage of your training. Don't put it off any longer. Don't let fear of the unknown keep you running in place any longer than you have to. You're already unhappy. Take the leap. What have you got to lose? More unhappiness? My guess is that in a few months you will say to yourself, "Why didn't I do this earlier?"

Just don't ask me to find your calling for you. I only write here.

CHAPTER 11

YOUR MENTOR WON'T TELL YOU EVERYTHING.

I never liked the word mentor because it conjures up an unrealistic YODA-like character. Mentors aren't all-knowing beings. They are simply seasoned advisors or teachers. You ask their advice and hopefully they can help you avoid the quicksand they've already fallen into. But they can't tell you everything you need to know because they are not YOU. You might not make the same decisions they would. And they have forgotten at least half of what they went through themselves. Nevertheless, you should take a mentors advice, swish it around in your mind, distill it, and use only what feels right, for YOU, at the time. Keep mentors in perspective. They sweat and bleed just like you do. They aren't career magicians.

That said, I still think you should seek them out. They are better than consultants because they have useful experience and love to talk about it. And, they'll do it for free! A good mentor will not only show you the way but might actually be able to open a few doors for you.

Where do you find a suitable mentor? Join a trade association; people who do the same thing you do. Network with anybody and everybody who might know more than you do. Read the trade magazines and call up someone who wrote an interesting article. Potential mentors are busy but many of them are waiting for someone to pay attention to them.

In the chapter, "Consultants Are Scams," you'll hear about a comedy coach/mentor I hired named Jim Richardson. For now, let me just say that he was a good mentor because he taught me specifically what I needed to know to go to the next professional level in my field. However, he couldn't write the jokes for me. I had to do that because it was all about ME! In fact, I'm not even sure Jim had a sense of humor. Regardless, he was a comedy scientist and I learned a bundle from him. So much so that I became dependent on him for every move I made. When I ran out of money and couldn't afford to keep paying for his expertise, I panicked. I still had so much more to learn. What's a comic to do?

Getting cut off from my mentor taught me two lessons. (1) Mentors that charge you money are called consultants and...(2) At some point you have to go it alone.

The comedy team of Mack & Jamie were great mentors to me. And, they were free! As comedians, they have the most reliably funny act I have ever seen. Audiences (comedy club and corporate worldwide) love them because they flat out "kill" every night.

I met them when I was their opening act at the *Seattle Comedy Underground*. We hit it off and they liked my act. So, when I asked them if they would introduce me to club owners in Los Angeles, they couldn't have been more kind. They opened doors for me at *The Ice House, The Improv, The Comedy Store*, and *The Comedy Magic Club*; all major venues that served as a showcase to give me a leg up. Mack & Jamie would listen to my routines and take time to help me (the struggling beginner) with my jokes. For instance, I had this bit about shaving. "I tried the Norelco rotary razor but at the end of the month when I went to clean it - there were no whiskers in there. I think those tiny little blades just spin around real fast and screw the whiskers right back in."

Mack & Jamie watched me and suggested I add another line to set up the joke. "I bought the rotary razor because I have trouble dispensing the right amount of shaving cream. I barely kiss the button with my finger and I end up with enough foam to shave a Yak!" A great addition.

I can't thank them enough.

What did they have to gain by helping me? Nothing. I had no power to do anything for them, at that time. Since then, I have spilled their names to corporate clients every chance I get.

Then came John Powell; an honest talent agent, manager, and mentor. I called him the Velvet Hammer because he was nice but tough.

John was (and is) a famous manager of national entertainers from the Pacific Northwest. In fact, besides musical acts, he managed the Northwest's most famous comedian, Pete Barbutti. Pete has countless hours of national exposure on all the major network talk shows. He has worked all of the big casinos and accompanied Johnny Carson on *The Tonight Show* at least once a month. To me, John Powell was the guy who had "connections." He could open big fat money-filled doors. I figured that was exactly what I needed; a major-league manager like John Powell!

One problem.

John wouldn't take my calls.

And, he wouldn't listen to my comedy tapes.

People who knew John said he thought I was too "green." Translation: not funny enough. I pursued him for over three years. Finally, one of his comedy clients, Mike Neun, gave me John's home address and I sent John a "cookie bouquet." You know, the big, chunky chocolate chip cookies on a stick? I enclosed a note that said. "John, I know I have been bothering you about representing me. If you have decided I'm not ready, then at least enjoy these delicious cookies as a token of my appreciation. However, if you DO want to sign me, please don't eat the poison cookies."

He called me the next day and said that was the first time I made him laugh. He immediately added me to his roster. Thanks to John, I was able to start working casinos like *Harrah's* in Reno, Lake Tahoe and Atlantic City. He also set it up for me to be represented by the powerful William Morris Agency. His contacts lifted me to another level.

Did I always listen to John's valuable advice? Only about 50% of the time. I respected John immensely but he wasn't a stand up comedian. And while he could give me the benefit of his show biz experience, ultimately it was ME who had to stand up in front of 200-20,000 strangers and get the laughs.

Then again, I should have listened to him when he said, "I don't care how much money they're paying. Don't do the Hells Angels BBQ."

IT'S ALWAYS ABOUT YOU:

Do you have a mentor? You don't? Do you know where to find one? Who would make a good mentor candidate? Do your research and get one. And when you have one, don't be afraid to ask your mentor for favors and connections. "Who you know" really matters. Finally, even though your mentor has experience and wisdom, listen to YOURSELF first. YOU are the one who has to live with your decisions.

CHAPTER 12

NETWORKING ONLY WORKS HALF THE TIME.

Networking: The term used for sucking up to people who you think can help you. It's much different than mentoring in that networking usually focuses on your peers. But you should realize networking won't work every time you need it. Unfortunately, we are brainwashed to think that networking will make it easy for us to get what we want. Make enough "contacts" and you'll have a key to get through any locked door, right? By now, you know the world doesn't work that easily. It's not enough to make friends and collect contacts. Chances are, these people won't (or can't) help you when you need help. Why? Because of timing, circumstances, selfishness...shall I go on? In networking with someone you see as valuable to your career, remember this. YOU are not THEIR number one priority. THEY are their number one priority. In order to help you, your contacts have to want to take time out their busy day. They also have to be in a position to help; and still know the valuable OTHER people, at the exact time you need their help. Furthermore, they have to secretly believe you won't screw up their good thing by helping. Oh sure, lots of people will tell you they "spoke on your behalf" or turned it over to the right person or any other lie that will get them off the responsibility hook. You've probably done it yourself.

As you will read in another chapter, I was down and out shortly after my big time TV success. I was desperate and really needed help. But I can't tell you how many times I asked my "friends" for a job, a referral, or for a break of any kind. Most of my contacts made excuses or lied to me. Some just didn't even bother to return my calls. How could that happen? I was a nice guy. I didn't step on people on the way up. I figured they didn't want to be associated with failure.

I'll go you one better. Mort Sahl made millions in the 60's as a political comedian. He has been a joke writer for (4) presidents. And, was even Paul Newman's Best Man at his wedding to Joanne Woodward. He knew absolutely everyone in show business and politics. Mort had amazing contacts. I'm talking about Warren Beatty, Sidney Pollock, Robert Redford, Sidney Poitier, and Mike Ovitz. His famous and powerful person list is too long to mention. But, when Mort put his comedy career on hold to join Jim Garrison in the Kennedy assassination investigation, his contacts all but evaporated. Mort had a very long, dry spell of no work because nobody wanted to be guilty by association. I take that back. One person showed interest. Woody

Allen. Another outcast. Woody has always believed in Mort's talent and stepped up to help resuscitate his career. Thanks to Woody and his manager, Jack Rollins, Mort has recently appeared on *The David Letterman Show*, *The Larry King Show*, and many others. Brilliant as ever, Mort is creating a brand new, and very enthusiastic fan base. Mort told me he read a magazine article quoting Woody as saying, "Mort Sahl changed my life." After several years apart, Woody ran into Mort, hugged him and said, "Can you change it back?"

So, keep that in mind. The "Outcast Club" sticks together. When you're down, look to others who have been there. They'll return your calls.

Now, to keep the glass half full, you can look forward to the other half of the time when networking actually pays off.

So how do you do it? It's not just about asking for favors. It's about knowing who to ask and when. First of all, stop being shy about talking to people when you're on the airplane, waiting in line, at conventions, wherever. Exchange business cards. There is no guarantee these people will ever return your call but your Palm Pilot should be up to its memory cache with experts and specialists. Someday they just might want to talk.

After a show one time, I gave out my business card to a starched young man at a carpet convention. He said he wanted to be comedian but never had the nerve. We exchanged a few jokes and off he went. Seven years later, I got a call from the president of a big sign company who said, "I wanted to hire you earlier but I was only a sales manager when I met you at the carpet convention, seven years ago."

Ken Kragen wrote a wonderful book titled, *Life is a Contact Sport.* Ken is a personal manager of storied fame in Hollywood. He has managed the careers of Kenny Rogers, Burt Reynolds, Trisha Yearwood, and Travis Tritt; to name a few. He makes it an obsession to know every person he ever meets. He gets the correct spelling of their name, their occupation, family members, who they know, etc. He even works hard at keeping track of their careers. If they change companies, Ken knows about it and sends a card. Consequently, he has an endless reference resource for whatever endeavor he wants to tackle. When Kenny Rogers wanted to get into the restaurant business, Ken knew a chicken magnate, made the call and the rest is *Kenny Rogers Roasters* history.

Networking pays off. If you're lost, ask for directions. Get on the phone, get in the car, write a letter, email, or knock on a door...but Ask! Success doesn't go looking for timid people.

Here's another great tip I learned from my friend, Rand Rosenberg. Rand had an amazingly successful career on Wall Street as an investment banker. Those big time multi-zillion dollar deals are often consummated by those with the right information at the right time. Rand did something very smart. He not only networked with the deal makers, but also with the second and third tier people. The folks who aren't in the limelight but hear what's going on. Whenever Rand needed to know the real pulse of the deal, he'd contact his stable of confidants; the people who were deemed insignificant in the actual deal but whose eyes and ears saw and heard everything.

Comedian and *Tonight Show* host, Jay Leno, uses a similar technique. In 1989, Jay and I were both working at *Harrah's* in Reno, Nevada. Then we would hang out during the day searching for the best cheeseburgers in town. Invariably, he would have to take a break to do an interview with a local High School or Junior High School newspaper reporter. Jay said, "You never know who they might end up working for." Sure enough, many of those same young journalists became writers for Vanity Fair, People, Esquire, The New York Times, you name it. And guess who they always give plenty of publicity ink to? Their "friend" Jay Leno.

By the way, as you are collecting people, make sure they know how to contact YOU in case THEY need some help someday.

IT'S ALWAYS ABOUT YOU:

Are you making contacts? Who do you already know? Are you keeping their contact information updated? You may not need these people now but you will. If your job is truly terminal, you better have a full Rolodex (er, Palm Pilot) to turn to. Better yet, if your boss asks you to find a chicken magnate, a radial tire genius, an Appalachian oral surgeon, or a Jeep salesman you can trust, you'll have your butt totally hooked up.

CHAPTER 13

YOUR FIRST IDEA USUALLY STINKS.

Never settle for your first decent idea. To date, that only worked for Amadeus Mozart. Mortals like us can't afford the luxury of settling for our first idea.

Too many times in your life your work will be judged on its first impression. Make sure your effort is as razor sharp as you can hone it. Raise the bar on yourself. Don't accept your first notion or your run at a solution. You can always improve on your idea. No writer, producer, or top business executive I know accepts their first draft as their best work. They squeeze the juice out of every possibility in search of originality and excellence.

I'll show you what I mean. Here is an example of a joke I wrote after I saw the 'Texas Chain Saw Massacre' movie. It took on several different incarnations before I nailed the right combination of attitude, point of view, and maximum laugh value. Ladies and gentlemen...The Chain Saw Joke.

First Draft: Where I grew up, in the rugged Pacific Northwest, a man chasing a woman with a chain saw meant dinner was late. (Mildly amusing but mean - got groans from women)

Second Draft: I watched that Texas Chain Saw Massacre movie and thought, "Hey, that guy is using my Dad's saw." (Pretty good laugh but the perspective wasn't twisted enough)

Third Draft: When I went to the Texas Chain Saw Massacre movie I wondered if anyone knew that was a phony saw the guy was using. The chain was making noise but it wasn't moving. (Not only is this NOT a joke, it got very far away from the best and more obscure observation)

Final Draft: Remember that Texas Chain Saw Massacre movie? It was just a normal movie to you guys. But in the Pacific Northwest we watched at it and said, "Can you believe they're using a McCulloch 210?"

That version works every time. Always a big Laugh. It is specific and draws attention to the absurdity of focusing on the wrong elements of the movie.

When our comedy writing team at *Almost Live* (Seattle TV show) would come up with a new comedy bit, we'd always ask ourselves, "It seems funny but is it original enough to win an Emmy Award?" Emmy Awards are given for innovation and outstanding achievement. And, if we didn't think our "bit" was unusual or funny enough, we'd usually move on. We never settled for ordinary. We strove (is that a real word?) for the extraordinary. By the time I left, our little local TV show had won over 30 of those little gold statues.

Ignore those people who say your first instinct is usually the best. That's just plain ignorant when you are writing, speaking or making presentations. "Winging it" is absolutely suicidal. Everybody needs to re-write, edit, and rewrite it again until it's worth reading.

Just think. If Moses had kept those tablets to himself just a little longer, he could rewritten them, come up with at least 30 more, and gotten an author credit. I'M KIDDING! Jeez, lighten up.

IT'S ALWAYS ABOUT YOU:

When was the last time you had to write a dynamic proposal or explain your latest great idea? Did you exhaust all of the possibilities or did you go with your first thought? Why did you settle? Jammed for time? Didn't want to spoil your pretty presentation folder? What would have happened if you had spent another half an hour on it? What would have happened if you let someone else read it before you turned it in? Makes you wonder if your competition spent an extra 30 minutes on their proposal and landed the business, doesn't it? Be clear, precise, and thorough and your work will be recognized for its attention to detail and excellence.

Oh, so that's how people get raises?

CHAPTER 14

I PRAY YOU ARE SHORT, FAT & BALD.

You think I'm kidding?

Play along with me for a moment and throw out the popular wisdom that, "Tall, handsome or beautiful people usually get better jobs and are offered better opportunities. They make better first impressions and companies love to hire them as front men and women." To add insult to injury, I read in USA TODAY (9-5-02) about how obese people are discriminated against and earn less because of their appearance. Obese women make even less than fat men because a man has to get REALLY fat in order to be considered unsightly by other men. A woman only has to be 30 pounds overweight to lose front row exposure at the important client meetings. A sad statement about our image conscience society, right?

Well, when I'm out there on the lecture circuit, I'm face to face with sometimes hundreds of front line employees and I've seen short, overweight, bald people win lots of awards. I've seen less than attractive men and women consistently climb to the top of the sales game and manage the biggest and best companies.

What accounts for this paradox?

Is the press is lying to sell papers?

Here's my theory. I agree that good-looking people have advantages. Good-looking people have been good looking for a long time. They have had an easier time getting the jobs they want. And they may have had entry into corporate circles where the less attractive folks have had to wait in the lobby. But it can also make the pretty people lazy. They assume customers and clients like doing business with a handsome face and they use it to their advantage. Some even flirt. Gasp!

Heavy, bald, short and not-ready-for-the-runway model type people know this and, in my opinion, work twice as hard. They don't spend their lunch hours searching for a vegetarian restaurant. They don't spend money on nose jobs and tanning salons. They don't live in fear of their careers vanishing if their looks start to fade. They are probably not dating shallow, slow witted, vain model types who take up their time, money and energy. They focus on the work at hand and get really good at it. And, we all know that short men overcompensate in the workplace to make more money for one reason only. To get chicks! And it works. There are plenty of women who are turned on by power and money. So turned on that they will overlook (literally) a 5' 5" bald man if he has a sense of humor, is a good provider and potentially excellent father. And for the unattractive women who work hard and achieve great things, they generally value character over curb appeal and usually pick better mates. Plus, they possess higher self-esteem knowing they don't need a man to support them. Good, decent men notice that and are drawn to their independence and success.

Everybody wins.

Danny DeVito & Dr. Ruth have done pretty well for themselves, don't you think? Even Napoleon was on a roll for awhile.

IT'S ALWAYS ABOUT YOU:

Are you SO concerned about how you look that you spend more time on your appearance than you do improving your work skills? Are the less good looking people running circles around you at work? Have you been humble or arrogant? Is anything wrong with your priorities? Stop looking at yourself in the mirror for a minute and answer these questions.

CHAPTER 15

WITH ANY LUCK, YOU'LL BE A FLUKE.

One of my oldest and dearest friends, Bill Nye, The Science Guy, will probably never let me drive his EV-1 electric car again when he reads that I put him in the fluke category. I say that knowing full well that Bill Nye, the Science Guy, IS the real deal. A true genius. How could he qualify as a fluke? How could that be luck? After all, Bill really is a Cornell graduate who studied under Carl Sagan. He knows more than you or I will ever know about earth, sea, and space science. As a reward, he gets huge bucks speaking all over the world on those subjects. I'd argue that Bill Nye is a fluke because, even with all that natural pedigree, I don't think Bill would have thought of the Science Guy idea by himself.

But shockingly, I did.

Yes, I was the person who came up with the idea to call Bill Nye, "The Science Guy!" I wish I could say it was a bolt of inspirational lightning. But it was out of sheer panic.

When we met, Bill was winning Steve Martin look-a-like comedy contests. He loved performing comedy and would have done anything to quit his full time aerospace engineer job at Boeing for a career in show business. As a stand up comedian, some nights he was brilliant. Other nights, he'd bomb just like the rest of us.

I think he was inconsistent because he studied the science of comedy like a lab experiment. Instead of honing the material he already had, he was more interested in creating and testing the success rate of "new" material. Of course, that's what scientists do.

Regardless, we all thought Bill was brilliantly quirky and we hired him as a writer/performer on our NBC television show, *Almost Live.* He would come to the pitch meetings, make us laugh, and usually convince us to put his funnier ideas on the air.

Aside from acting in sketches, Bill created or co-created such popular recurring characters as, "The High Fivin' White Guys" and "Speedwalker" (a crime fighting fast walker). But there was something else quite odd about Bill. We noticed that a lot of his source material came from the various science trade magazines that kept falling out of his worn backpack. This guy was reading science magazines for fun!? Science was obviously his passion and his semi-secret hobby. Nonetheless, we gave him endless grief for it.

Soon, we would find a way to exploit it.

One day, Geraldo Rivera had to cancel an appearance on our show due to the flu. That meant we had an emergency six-minute guest slot to fill.

In desperation, I turned to Bill and pleaded, "Look, if we put you in a lab coat could you do some kind of funny experiment?" He looked around the room, smiling. I kept riffing. "We'll introduce you as Bill Nye, The Science Guy, and you can dazzle the audience with some kind of funny science gag. It will be great!

That night, Bill was incredible. He "roasted" marshmallows in (minus) 325-degree liquid nitrogen, ate one, and steam came out of his nose! Hilarious! Another time, he built a hovercraft from a leaf blower. He was a hit!

Every time Bill made an appearance, he was absolutely hysterical. "Science Rules" became his trademark phrase and we got lots of letters wondering when he was going to be on the show. More startling was that he made our hard core comedy audience actually care about science.

Looking back, it's ironic that the Science Guy was born from panic and not planning. It was a fluke that we needed to fill time that night. To Bill's credit, it was the broad knowledge of his passion that enabled him to combine science with comedy and turn it into gold. It was even luckier that we could find a lab coat from a nearby nurses uniform store.

The timing and confluence of those events turned out to be the mother lode for Bill. This fluke propelled Bill into a breakout TV star that could leave his day job in the dust.

Bill threw himself into the study of comedy and science and created an Emmy Award winning TV series that is shown several times a day - all over the blue planet. He became the new Mr. Wizard!

Teachers still use his monthly newsletter and web site in classrooms, every day.

And, it may never have happened if Geraldo had signed up for flu shot.

IT'S ALWAYS ABOUT YOU:

What do you have in your bag of tricks that, if viewed differently, could change your life? Do you have hidden skills that you haven't been using? Scribble down a quick inventory of your talents. Could you apply your hobbies and passions to your work life in some way? What gets you excited? What magazines do you read for fun? If you could change your life in some way, what would you change? What's stopping you? If you don't think you can do it, think about Bill Nye. What made Bill world renowned, never even occurred to him.

CHAPTER 16

STOP TAKING CREDIT FOR YOUR "PHENOMENAL SUCCESS."

So, you say *your* success wasn't a fluke? You say that it was through dedication and diligence that your "plan" finally came true? I'm not buying it. And, I have other startling news. You don't control the universe.

(Again, please read chapter #27 about "plans")

If you're lucky, you will experience one or two big "hits" in your career. By that I mean you will enjoy a phenomenal success by some product you helped create, a service you provided, or a promotion you launched. But don't kid yourself, you can't take all the credit. A lot of planets had to line up.

A phenomenal hit isn't about YOU. It has to do with luck, timing and the general population. It's the public's appetite that determines a success like *The Sopranos*, *Viagra*, and even *Pop Tarts*. If you can tap into their needs at the right time, your idea will explode. But remember it was the public that made your idea a phenomenon; not you.

My *Almost Live* cohorts and I worked diligently to come up with funny and innovative approaches to draw viewers to our upstart TV show. Every idea flopped. Even the good ones were met with medium to luke-warm response. And, these people were as bright and creative as any gaggle of Mensa members. But, the right combination kept evading us. Worse. Ratings were slipping.

Then, we landed on the notion to change the state song of Washington to *Louie, Louie*. (Actually, I am not exactly sure whom on our TV staff thought of the idea but I have been taking credit for it for years).

Here's what happened.

I went on our weekly TV show and announced that we were going to lead a campaign to change the Washington State song from the unknown, *Washington My Home*, to the rock hit, *Louie, Louie*. We passed out *Louie, Louie* buttons and I even went to the state capitol in Olympia to plead with the state legislators.

Unwittingly, we'd hit a nerve.

The groundswell of public support for this silly idea was staggering. 15,000 people showed up, during a workday, to support *Louie, Louie* for the state song. Paul Revere and the Raiders showed up to play the song. So did The Kingsmen (who made the song famous) and The Wailers. Oh, and so did everyone in the news media.

We were instantly famous.

In some form or another, the *Louie, Louie* campaign was in the press for 261 straight days. We even got the Dubious Achievement Award from Esquire Magazine. A full-on bonafied phenomenon was taking place. Everywhere I went people wanted to know about the campaign. As I mentioned earlier, Dick Clark had me on his national *TV's Bloopers and Practical Jokes* show to talk about the Capitol rally. It was huge!

With one major snag.

The original author of *Washington My Home* was still alive...and she was pissed.

Helen Davis, 86, lived in Pasco, Washington and had also been in the middle of the press melee. What did she think of these upstart TV boys who threatened to unseat her song? She demanded equal broadcast time. She went on a Spokane radio station and said, "If that Ross Shafer wants to change the state song to *Louie, Louie*, he might as well change the state flower to marijuana."

Harsh words.

I went on TV the next week and said, "Look Helen, one campaign at a time."

The downside is this. Anyone who has ever been involved in a phenomenon convinces himself he was the one who was responsible.

I am around it all the time. When a TV show, record, or movie is a hit, big money runs to anyone associated with "the project" - hoping to capture lightning in a bottle, one more time. Worse, some of these people start believing their own press clippings, jump ship, and are lured by the competition to bring the magic with them.

As lucrative and flattering as it is, don't fall into this trap. Just because you had a phenomenon once doesn't guarantee that it will happen again.

After our *Louie, Louie* success, I started getting offers to "consult" with advertising agencies who were looking for the next big thing in clothing, weed killers, automobiles...as if I knew what that was going to be?! I had plenty of ideas but there was no way I could predict their success. It wasn't up to me. The public always dictates what will be popular. They determine if my jokes are funny and if your products will sell...and how much they are willing to pay.

One more story about how important you are to the success of the project.

Remember the TV show *Fantasy Island*? It was the TV show where Herve Villechaize would chant, "Da Plane, boss, Da Plane?" There is a story around Hollywood that after *Fantasy Island* was a hit, Herve went to Ricardo Montelbahn (star & Exec. Producer) and said, "Ricardo, I am a big star. Everywhere I go people are chanting my catch phrase, Da Plane, Da Plane, and I want more money. If I don't get a big raise I am leaving the show." Ricardo reportedly said, "I understand and I agree. *Fantasy Island* is holding you back. Good luck, my friend."

THIS TIME IT'S _NOT_ ALWAYS ABOUT <u>YOU</u>:

Have you ever been associated with a "hit?" Have you thought it was your sole brainstorm that broke it wide open? Learn a lesson in humility. Relish the moment but give credit to the public who bought the product or idea. Then, go to work on the next one. You can't live a lifetime on one victory. Although some people try. There is a saying in Hollywood that it is easier to make a killing than a living. A career is built on longevity; many victories accompanied by even more failures.

In the meantime, if someone wants to buy you a drink, give you an award, or boost your paycheck, thank him and enjoy the moment.

Just remember. I'm watching to make sure your head doesn't explode from swelling.

CHAPTER 17

YOUR DREAMS ALWAYS LOOK BETTER IN THE WINDOW.

For many years I was guilty of the "If only" syndrome. Actually, I'm not even sure if it is an official syndrome. I just know that I would always say to myself, "If only I made $10,000 a month" - "If only I didn't have to work 9-5." - "If only I knew so-and-so." I'm sure you've had many of the same thoughts.

One of my "if only" dreams was to perform my stand up comedy act at the big casino showrooms in Las Vegas or Atlantic City. I'd been slogging it out in dirty, smoke filled taverns (posing as comedy clubs) and making the jump from little bars and nightclubs to Casinos is huge for an entertainer; both in status and pay.

When I finally got there (as the opening act for Three Dog Night, Crystal Gayle, Eddie Rabbit, Dionne Warwick and others) I found that every venue hid a new pit of quicksand; waiting and churning specifically for me.

One such night at Harrah's in Lake Tahoe, I accidentally stood on Crystal Gayle's floor length hair; snapping her neck back as she tried to take the stage. Her manager/husband fired me, immediately.

Another time, at Caesar's Palace in Las Vegas, I got bold enough to write the following joke for country singer, Eddie Rabbitt. "It's hard when you are a kid and Rabbitt is your real last name. It was especially hard for my sister Bunny." Cute and funny, I thought. He was hesitant to try it but I begged him. I knew it would work.

That night he delivered the joke like this. "You know, Rabbitt is my real last name. My sister's name is Bunny Rabbitt."

It got no response. No laugh. No hiss. No sound. Period.

Of course not! He butchered the all-important order of the words. Regardless, he thought I was a hack joke writer and I never worked with him again.

But, my all time worst job happened in the main showroom of John Ascquaga's Nugget in Sparks, Nevada. This was a really sweet gig for which I was being paid a lot of money at the time ($7,500/week) to open the show for The Bellamy Brothers. I remember thinking. "Man, I am officially in show business, now!"

Nobody Moved Your Cheese!

When I went down for the afternoon sound check, the gigantic stage manager (former *Foghat* roadie) grabbed me by the scruff of my neck and said, "Here's how it works. Bertha (a 38 year old - 8,000 pound elephant) goes on first. She does a "tight nine" and then you go on." A tight nine? That means Bertha will do a short nine-minute act consisting of balancing and rearing up; all to the tune of, *The Elephant Walk.* Not belly splitting - but pretty impressive when a giant elephant is stomping one of its 24-inch diameter hooves six inches from your pasta.

For six straight shows we were a hit.

Bertha does her short routine.

I'd go on and get nice laughs for the next twenty minutes.

The Bellamy Brothers closed the show with *Let Your Love Flow*, getting their usual standing ovation. We all ate together. It was so awesome to be in show business.

However, on the seventh (and last) night, the stage manager calls the phone in my dressing room with the following news. "Bertha is a bit plugged. She hasn't had a proper "movement" in about nine days and we're wondering what you would like to do about it? Me? Folks, I read the paper and I watch CNN...but I am certainly not your guy to advise anyone on Pachyderm gastrointestinal disorders.

As if I knew the answer, I said, "Well, Bertha has been on stage for over 30 years. She's probably been through everything. Why don't we let her go on." The stage manager smiled accidentally.

I couldn't have given worse "advice."

That night, Mighty Bertha was visibly uncomfortable. She winced as she pirouetted around the stage in her size 1,000 tutu. But being the trouper she is, Bertha rose to the occasion and after nine floor-thumping minutes, she got her usual thunderous applause and lumbered off.

But whatever happened to Bertha on stage must have dislodged something.

Because as soon as the curtain closed, backstage Bertha relaxed.

The sound could only be compared to the Navy leaving port. You see, when an elephant "Severs the Wind" it is LOUD and NOT invisible. If you are an 8,000 pound elephant, your daily grub is 200 pounds of hay, wheat and barley. With that diet, an elephant happens to innocently manufacture a dusty olive colored fog. That "fog" is now filling the backstage area. Everyone within a 30-foot radius is choking. The stagehands turn on giant fans to help dissipate the fog. At the same time, I hear my name being announced, "Ladies and gentlemen, the comedy of Ross Shafer." The red velvet curtain opens. And, with the wind machines at my back, "the fog" and me are driven into the audience. As you might imagine, people in the first four rows were taken aback by the unexpected eye-watering gale. Do you think any of them deduced that wind belonged to Bertha?!

I didn't work at the Nugget for nearly three years.

Now I make it a rule to dream the nightmare, first. If I can live with that, I continue the dream.

IT'S ALWAYS ABOUT YOU:

What do you dream about? If you achieved your dream, would you expect the reality to be as wonderful as your dream? It won't be. Don't believe the people who try to talk you into "the perfect situation." No situation is perfect. It's almost impossible for the dream to live up to itself. Be realistic. Expect "the perfect situation" to be something that has blemishes and unpredictable surprises. Expect adversity and be joyous when you don't have to deal with it. Even when things go wrong you'll be much wiser for the experience.

I think it was the great meteorologist, Willard Scott who said, "Weathered storms are never as big the next time." Either that or I made it up and used his name to add some funny credibility.

CHAPTER 18

RENT YOUR DREAMS BEFORE YOU BUY THEM.

Naturally, there are times when you see a happy person who seems to have everything and you think, "I hate him but I want to be *him*. I deserve *his* life. I want *her* hobbies. Then, I'd be just as happy as *they* are! No! Happier!!"

Ok, fine. Rent their dream before you buy it. Give it a test drive and see if it even fits. If that means that you take night classes or seminars to learn a new skill suited to that dream, do it. What's the risk?

I love my Mom. And my Mom loved horses. Nothing seemed to make her happier than riding them, talking about them, and looking at pictures of horses. So, as a boy I loved horses, too. As luck would have it, when I was twelve, we moved near a pasture with horses. I made friends with the stable manager and he let me feed and ride a Shetland Pony named, King. I didn't care that King bit people and never learned to gallop. He was a horse. I read every book I could about the care and feeding of these graceful creatures and my full time dream was to eventually land a job around horses.

When I was in college, I badgered a trainer at the local racetrack and he finally relented. My job started out as the barn boy. Shoveling and dumping was my job description. But I worked hard, wore nose plugs and waited for a valued "track assistant" position. That would be heaven. Rubbing shoulders with thoroughbred race horses. I dreamt about the Starting Gate. The Jockeys. The betting. I loved it all.

The big day finally came. The stable manager said his track assistant had walked off the job and wondered if I thought I could handle it. Was he kidding? And leave stable boy duty? Show me the ponies!

This was a case of the dream definitely looking better in the shop window. My "glamorous" track assistant job was to follow the winning horse, after the race, and collect the horse's urine for drug testing. The mechanics of that job are executed by taping a plastic cup on the end of a broom handle...follow the horse...and wait.

First of all, an Arabian Stallion never stands still. They are perpetually hyper. Sometimes the horse is so wired after winning a race that he won't pee for hours. Other times, he will just kick you in the chest because he doesn't like having a broom handle wavering near his penis. I'd rented the dream and turned it back in after two weekends. Then, I turned my focus on learning new skills that didn't involve collecting urine.

IT'S ALWAYS ABOUT YOU:

What dream job have you always wanted? How did it look in the window? Did you try it? How did it turn out? Did you acquire extra training or skills in order to give it a fair chance? See, that can be a problem. The world keeps changing. Your academic education might not be able to keep pace with those changes. And your skills might not be transferable to the dream in the window. A specialized job (even Urine collection) requires specialized skills. Get the training. Take classes. Attend seminars. Hire a coach. Talk to a mentor. Every hour of education puts one more arrow in your employment quiver. My dad used to say, "If you stop learning, you stop earning."

Don't let a little extra night school or weekend seminars keep you from finding a career that wakes you up before the alarm clock goes off.

CHAPTER 19

THE (7) HABITS OF HIGHLY SNEAKY PEOPLE WHO WILL SCREW YOU.

This single chapter is more important than the whole, *"7 Habits of Highly Successful People"* book written by Steven R. Covey. His book was a valiant effort to encourage you to behave like successful people behave. But again, their circumstances are not YOURS. The best you can do is copy someone else's habits. Hopefully, not their bad ones. And even if you faithfully practice the habits of successful people, throughout the course of your life plenty of people will try to screw yours up.

In fact, some of them are staying up nights plotting new ways to sabotage you. Somebody out there doesn't like you.

Somebody out there wants your job or they want you to quit. Others just want to make you look bad so they can look better. The shocking truth is that, these days, that kind of behavior isn't considered shameful.

What happened to goodness and ethics? When you and I weren't looking, decency became unpopular. Edgy, bold, vindictive and outrageous behavior took its place.

All you have to do is remember the TV show *Survivor* to see what this country has become. That TV show actually glamorizes and rewards devious behavior with a $1,000,000 dollar cash prize. These clowns form phony alliances with "friends" and then laughingly betray them. Another TV show called *Dog Eat Dog* rewarded sneaky, abhorrent behavior.

Yet another, *The Mole*, was a program that featured a spy who won money for betraying other contestants.

Other TV series like *Jerry Springer* feed on watching the pain of wrecked families; even cheering a violent family explosion. It makes me ashamed of my TV producer peers. How have they been successful in selling the idea that it is normal to screw your buddy?

From my vantage point, it seems that getting through life has become so vicious that we have adopted a survivalist attitude. A sort of, "If you aren't going to help me, then get the hell out of my way."

So, how can you prevent people from screwing you over?

You can't.

But you *can* be cautious of the work alliances you form. Here are the seven habits of people who will screw you. (There are more, but seven should keep you busy for a while.)

1) <u>*They gossip about your mutual friends behind their backs.*</u>

Oh yeah, it's really funny when Darla pulls you aside to gossip about Cathy's disastrous family life. She also makes fun of her vocabulary, her hair style, her clothes, and the loser men she dates. But, you aren't in a secured cone-of-silence with Darla. Darla is saying the same things about you behind your back - probably telling Cathy about your drunken tattoo night. Would she really do that? Yes. People who gossip can't stop. You are tomorrow's gossip and Darla will deny it if you confront her; which is why it won't do you any good to confront her. The solution? Keep gossip to yourself and be too busy to chat with her when she calls.

<u>2) *They only call you when they need something.*</u>

Selfish people couldn't care less about you. They will smile as they use you for advice, to cover their ass, or to curry favor.

But the favors are never reciprocal. If backed into a corner, these people won't help you and will not be your ally. They may be the funniest people to invite to your party but they are the weasels who WON'T get out of bed to help you change a flat tire on a stormy night. Try not to get too close to these takers because you will expect too much and always be disappointed.

3) They deliberately misinterpret what you say or lie to cover their own butt.

I admire the characters in Mafia movies because those guys cover each other's back; every time. If you aren't in the Mafia, beware of acquaintances who don't have the same code of ethics.

If you get into a jam and your friend deliberately misstates what you know to be the truth, you know this person would jerk the rescue rope from your hands to save his/her slippery hide. They might even apologize to you, "What could I do, my back was against the wall and I could have lost my job. I'll make it up to you." You're sorry?   Me too. One chance is all I give these spineless half-wits. Whoever coined the old saying, "With friends like these, who needs enemies?" never saw a Mafia movie.

4) They build a case against you; cataloguing your mistakes.

In college, I became friendly with a guy named Mark Dix (a fake name but he will know who he is). We both worked for a retail clothing store in Yakima, Washington. I later moved to Seattle. We were great buddies and when Mark and his wife, Marta, wanted to move to Seattle, I got him a job at the same store where I was working. We even lived across the street from each other. Over the next year, he methodically built a fabricated case against me and I got fired. Mark was standing by to take my job. In retrospect, I knew Mark was dishonest and sneaky. He cheated at pool. He cheated on his wife. Other times, he would quiz me over and over about what I was doing. Then, misquote me and use it against me with the boss. Occasionally, I would walk around a corner and catch him halting a conversation with the boss. But he was my best friend, at the time, so I blindly blew it off. Don't be as dumb as I was. If you get suspicious for good reason, do something about it? And I think there is only one way to stop this sort of thing.

Never make friends with Mark Dix.

5) They build alliances with others to weaken you.

I used to have this joke in my act. "I work at an advertising agency and my co-workers are constantly trying to sabotage me. They keep letting me pitch my own ideas." The joke was borne from truth. My coworkers knew I was weak "on my feet" so they let me hang myself in meetings. My ineptness guaranteed that my corporate rise would spiral like a flushed toilet. Sure enough, almost anybody got promoted over me.

Woody Allen used to say something like, "Just because you're paranoid, don't let your paranoia convince you that people really aren't out to get you." Hey, if you are feeling left out, you probably are. Like buzzards circling their prey, you are probably the next one to be eaten. The solution is to divide and conquer. If you really care about staying where you are, break up the group. Worm your way into the only good hearted person and work your way out from there. Integrity, honesty, and truth are still your strongest weapons.

6) They steal your ideas.

There is outright theft of your sole idea. Then there is team theft. Huh? The "team" works together to solve problems, right? So how can it be stealing if the group created the "intellectual property?"

I'm talking about someone, on the team, who sees a window of opportunity and deliberately steals your ideas, your plan, your model, you're whatever for their personal gain. The major problem is that these jerks have no conscience about doing it. I love their rationale, "Look, it wasn't personal. It's just business."

Bullshit!

It's always personal when you rob someone's originality and call it your own! And, these people will do it over and over again as a normal way of doing business. If you spot them, change the locks on your brain and never let them look under the hood.

7) They are hot tempered to the point of irrationality.

This group is scary. They yell. They blow easily and you never know what they will say in the heat of the moment. Most likely, they will spit out whatever is meant to cause the most immediate pain. Which could be anything you may have uttered in confidence. They might not even mean to screw you. But they are hotheads and you could inadvertently get caught up in their backwash. Dire consequences may result. How can you fend off the loudmouth and the stupidly opinionated? Keep your thoughts to yourself. Don't give them ammunition that may be damaging or incriminating to you and your career.

IT'S ALWAYS ABOUT YOU:

Face it. There are plenty of snakes out there. They want what you have and they don't care what they have to do to get it. You can't stop them but you can be prepared for when they strike. It's just how an ugly segment of the world works. Who do you know that follows these descriptions? If you know who they are, disown them. Let them go. You will do just fine without them. That way, you won't be found guilty by slimy association.

DESPITE WHAT YOU'VE HEARD, THERE <u>ARE</u> SHORTCUTS TO SUCCESS.

CHAPTER 20

BACK UP YOUR LIES WITH THE TRUTH.

You want the fastest route to the top? Lie.

I'm totally serious. If you get offered an incredible job or business opportunity BEFORE you are ready to take it, look that person in the eyeballs and...lie.

I've done it a million times.

I'm not talking about lies to cover your butt from past lapses in judgement.

I'm talking about lying to challenge *yourself* to become truthful.

Confusing?

Look at it this way. How many times you been asked if you could take on a certain job - a task you hadn't done before - but would like to. My attitude was always this. If somebody had enough confidence to ask me, then I was going to take advantage of the opportunity. Therefore, I would always say, "YES!" and then figure out how to do the job, later. What about failing? I suppose it's a possibility but not for me. I simply don't consider failure an option. My method of operation was that if I asked enough people who knew; enlisted enough "battle tested' opinions, I couldn't screw up that badly. In fact, because I felt pressure to back up my lie with the truth, chances were better that I might end up doing the job very well. (one of the few theories I got right.)

When I became a working comedian, a local Seattle TV station had the ignorance to ask me if I could produce a 30-minute TV show. With great confidence I said, "YES!" So, they hired me. I HAD NO IDEA HOW TO PRODUCE A TV SHOW! But I didn't want to blow the opportunity. So, I spent the next three weeks calling people, reading books, watching TV shows, and learning how to do that job. I timed the segments. I timed the commercials, I saw where they inserted the graphics, where they put the furniture, who talked and when they talked. Every detail, minute-by-minute. Guess what? Three weeks later I was ready (complete with a hand picked team of professionals) to tackle the job.

I have done the same thing in my speaking career. Clients have asked, "Ross, can you do a 4 hour workshop on Overcoming the Fear of Public Speaking?" or "Do you have an hour of funny Customer Service stories?" or "Could you make a Human Resource training film teaching people to get along better?" Each time, I blurted out, YES! Truthfully, I only had a vague notion of how to pull these things off, at the time. But, the challenge and potential profit motivated me to back up my lies with the truth. The result was always better than I expected and I truthfully learned (or was coached on) everything I was being asked to do.

There is yet another scenario where I've forced myself to say, Yes. When I've spotted unique opportunities and asked MYSELF if I could do them. I have always said Yes, to myself; even when it was WAY out of my area of expertise...like the drug business. Not street drugs but drug store pharmaceuticals.

A few years ago, I noticed that a couple of drug companies offered free educational videos to accompany first time users of diabetes machines. I thought, "Why not offer a short informational video for other conditions?" So, I called a friend of mine, John Lloyd, who is an expert in the pharmaceutical business and asked him if he could identify some conditions, companies and drugs that might be candidates. He targeted companies who treated arthritis and hypertension and I made the inquires. Of course, these big companies didn't want to hear a pitch from a comedian. I mean, what did I know about their business? All I knew was that they made a lot of money and I wanted some of it. So John coached me, schooled me on the terminology, and tested me. Within a month I was in New Jersey with a 30-page script educating arthritis sufferers. Here I was, in a room with a group of master degreed pharmaceutical reps confidently yakking like I'd spent a lifetime in the drug business.

All because I said "Yes" to myself.

I walked out with a $230,000 order. To this day, they probably still think I missed my calling.

So, don't say NO too soon. We've all heard the famous Clint Eastwood Dirty Harry quote, "A man has got to know his limitations."

I completely disagree. Knowing your limitations could kill your chances of success - or even a new career. Saying you have limited skills in an area gives you an excuse to justify your fear. If you think you aren't capable of doing something, your attitude will guarantee it. But if you never give yourself a chance, how will you know? You have no idea what hidden skills you have. Skills you've talked yourself out of having.

Top executives are the worst at this.

Because I speak in public for a living, big league executives have hired me to coach them on their public speaking skills. The first thing they tell me is, "I gotta get some coaching because I am a terrible speaker. I just have to accept that I'm no good at it and have to figure out an easier way to stumble through the board meeting." That attitude forecasts failure; enabling the self fulfilling prophecy to come true. But after some basic coaching, they see dramatic improvements. Improvements that quash their old fearful notions, forever.

How many of you thought you would never be able to use a computer? How many of you thought you could never play a musical instrument? Trade stocks online? Plan a huge party or meeting?

Besides, what is the WORST CASE SCENARIO?

The worst case is that you really stink.

That's not bad. You've accomplished two things. (1) Now you aren't afraid, stunned, puzzled, or confused by the process.

(2) You can find someone really good at it and know how to measure his or her success.

I'm not against strategic alliances with somebody whose skill level is greater than mine. I just want to know what they are doing so they don't overcharge me for their expertise.

IT'S ALWAYS ABOUT YOU:

What have you said "No" to lately? Is it too late to go back and snag the opportunity? What if you said "Yes" to something that scared you? It won't be nearly as scary as you think; once you get your toes wet. I believe you can learn whatever you want to learn if you feel like putting in the hours. Believe in yourself. Then, as the Nike ads say, "Just Do it."

CHAPTER 21

THE FEAR OF PUBLIC SPEAKING IS HIGHLY OVERRATED.

I touched on this briefly in the last chapter regarding the executives who want public speaker coaching. But I truly think public speaking is one of the all time fastest shortcuts to success. Speaking well in public will accelerate your career; literally at the speed of sound. Look around your plant or office. Good talkers are looked upon as leaders and are getting the top money, right?

Is speaking in public scarier than waking up next to Anna Nicole Smith?

Scarier than being trapped in an elevator with James Carville?

Scarier than your "check engine light" flashing in the middle of the Mojave Desert?

Probably not. But being afraid to speak in public can hamstring your career. If you tip toe through life scared, you flat won't get very far. You will be passed over for promotions. Your company won't want you to represent them at important functions. You will lose too much weight and all of your teeth and hair will fall out. (Ignore the last (3) consequences)

If you give the impression of being scared in public situations, you won't inspire people and you'll never be an effective leader. And, if you are terrified to stand up and speak on behalf of your beliefs, then the rest of us won't respect you either.

Need any more reasons to get over your fear of public speaking? OK, here you go.

I usually meet the up-and-coming executives at their annual corporate conferences. Invariably, these young lions and lionesses must stand up, give a report, or address the troops. I can always tell who will wither and who will win; based on these podium performances. Just as in nature, the strong devour the weak. The weak usually are not at next year's conference.

I'll repeat. The fastest way to the top of your career is through your ability to speak well in large groups. You will be noticed and recognized. Furthermore, if you can "walk the talk," (which means if you can back up your claims with action) your career has no limits.

Can you do it? Yes! If I could do it, you most certainly can too.

I'm on stage for a living, now. But until my late 20's, I was stupifyingly frozen in fear by the thought of talking to groups.

Nobody Moved Your Cheese!

At my first job out of college, I had to give an ad campaign presentation to the large sales staff of the *Yard Birds Shopping Center* in Chehalis, Washington. I was the new guy and I was absolutely terrified. I tried to stall an extra week while I "gathered new data." One of the owners, Rich Gillingham, saw right through me, "Son, the fear of public speaking is highly overrated. I'm surprised most people still believe that old crock."

Hmm, I'd never heard it put like that before. Overrated? Haven't we been pummeled since birth that public speaking was the #1 fear of all time? I told him I always got really nervous if I had to address a group of strangers. He said, "How do you know you're nervous? Can you SEE your nerves under your skin?" I said, "No." Rich shot back, "Neither can we. Now, get out there." So, I scraped the cotton from my tongue and forged ahead. Amazingly, once I got started I was fine. It was the "getting started" part that pounded a hammer against my heart.

Rich was right. Nervousness is invisible to everybody but you. You are ON FIRE inside. Your heart is pounding. Your brain is muddled and your voice is quivering. Or, so you think. But from the outside, you look fine. You aren't shaking and your voice sounds exactly the same.

I'm not kidding.

In the late 80's, Johnny Carson had been on TV for 25 years. He played tennis several times a week and had a resting heartbeat of about 65 beats a minute. As a part of a routine physical exam, a doctor hooked Johnny up to a heart monitor; just prior to him going through that familiar Tonight Show curtain. Ed McMahon announced, "Heeerrres Johnny!" And

Johnny's heart rate jumped to 160 beats a minute! Clearly the sign of a nervous man, right? Out front, the audience saw a cool and collected Johnny Carson waltz through the curtain just as he had all of their lives. Remember, Johnny had been going through that same curtain, seeing the same staff people on the other side, performing in the same studio that had been his TV home for over two decades. And HE got nervous?

Of Course! If you don't get a little nervous, you're dead!

The point is this. Everybody feels anxious and nervous before speaking to a group. It's our hard-wired flight or fight response. Fight or flight is critical because it focuses your mind. If you were a caveman and a Velociraptor was about to chew on your throat, you would want to be focused. So, no matter how accomplished a speaker you become, you will always feel that adrenaline pump. That is your body telling you to get ready for your peak performance level. Embrace it. Expect it. You will be a far more aware and more passionate speaker because of it.

And while we're being honest, admit it. Some of your "fear" is that the audience won't like you. Believe me, they are on Your side. They want You to succeed. Some of them aren't even thinking about liking you one way or the other. They're thinking about how glad they are they aren't YOU at this moment!

How do you win them over? Just give them what they want; information, insight, inspiration, fun, or whatever. As long as you don't waste their time and are willing to give them something valuable for free, (information, advice, or balloons) they will love you.

How do you start talking? First, demand a proper introduction. Have someone introduce you or do it yourself. Have them brag about your credentials. A strong introduction gives you credibility and will give the audience a reason to listen to you.

What about jokes?

You don't have to "open with a good joke." That's a fallacy. I have heard so many speakers open with bad jokes - only to see them bury themselves. Unless you have a killer joke that works every time, don't tell it. A bad joke is almost unrecoverable.

And, don't tell a joke that is totally inappropriate for the occasion.

I was at a big nurse anesthetist's convention. No, they weren't big nurses. There were just a lot of them. Anyway, the speaker ahead of me said, "I just started dating a homeless woman. It's great because when the date was over, I could just drop her off anywhere." I secretly howled at the joke but it was the wrong crowd for the gag. These nurses treat homeless people every day and they hated this guy.

SIDE NOTE FOR THE GUYS: Women in general, don't laugh at the same crass jokes we men do. Women are especially sensitive to jokes where the "victim" in the joke gets hurt. Women identify with the victim of the joke and feel sorry for that person. Men don't have the same reaction. Men will say, "It's just a joke. The people in the joke aren't even real." That doesn't matter to some women. They are empathizing with the imaginary victim as if it happened to them. If you want to play it safe always make yourself the victim of the joke with self-deprecating humor. Women will always laugh at you getting hurt because they can see you're all right.

Instead of trying to be funny, just start by smiling and saying hello; a verbal handshake to the audience, so to speak. Then, bridge the gap between you and them by referring to the previous topic, the tasty lunch, the bad air conditioning, the speaker before you, or anything else that proves to the group that you were paying attention and that you care about them. Launching into your canned pitch without making a connection to the audience is a speaker's death warrant.

Above all, be yourself. Don't try to be a "speaker." Be YOU. Don't try to read big, fancy, powerful words from 3X5 cards. I'm talking about words that you would never use in your everyday life. I promise you, you won't remember these new words. And, because those words don't belong in your regular vocabulary your audience will smell it and eat you alive. Worse, they won't believe you and your credibility will be shot.

Here is a great story about just being you.

Five years ago, a major telephone company was changing CEO's and I was hired to do some executive speech coaching. The new CEO was a 45 year-old woman who wanted specifically to be, "more presidential." To her, this meant being more commanding, more in control, more dynamic. So, I watched some tapes of her previous speeches to get a sense of her style. I found her to be charming, real, engaging, and very warmly received. I encouraged her to capitalize on the attributes that already worked, tell more personal stories, and rally the troops by her own example. I reminded her that she already had the job! She didn't need to pretend to be anybody else. It worked. She is beloved to this day.

It happened to me. And, I even knew to look out for it.

I had already become a network TV host before I was offered the job to host the remake of *The Match Game* for ABC. I grew up loving *The Match Game* and *To Tell the Truth.* So when the producer of the *New Match Game*, Mark Goodson, (of Goodson/Toddman fame) selected me as his new host, naturally, I wanted to impress him.

After the first taping, I asked him how he thought it went. Mark acted puzzled and said, "Pretty good, I think. But who was hosting the show? I thought we hired Ross Shafer but he hasn't shown up yet." Whoa! He saw that I was acting like I thought a game show host should act. I wasn't being myself. Once I got ME back on track and hosted the show with MY personality, I was able to get the show cancelled within a year; as myself! (see, that's an example of self deprecating humor)

What about using notes? Avoid notes as if they are tainted with poison. Speak from your heart - not the page. You will move people if you can speak from your passions and true beliefs. Your true point of view will always be more convincing. If you have to use notes, just write down a few words that will jog your memory. Whatever you do, don't type out your speech verbatim. That will tempt you to read it and you will put us into a coma.

I have done a fair amount of public speaker coaching at Microsoft. The same folks who brought you the amazing Power

Point computer slide program. Invariably, my first task is to wean them from their own product. While Microsoft has revolutionized (and beautified) slide show presentations, many speakers rely too heavily on this electronic crutch. A popular complaint I've heard from hard-to-please meeting planners about other speakers is this: "Thanks for not using notes. I'm tired of paying big bucks for a speaker who just stands up there and reads his Power Point program." The same goes for using slides or other visual aids. If you must use them, make them short and to the point. Then elaborate by speaking from your heart. Also, pictures and video are always better than lots of small words on a screen. Statistics confuse most people and have been known to induce labor. If you have to give figures, use "ALMOST HALF" instead of 48.67%. Say "ONE THIRD" instead of 33.3%. The audience is thinking, "C'mon, we've just eaten a huge lunch, don't make us calculate!"

Ok, you've given your speech, talk, or presentation. How do you stop talking? How do you end it? Above all, DON'T end your speech by asking, "Does anybody have any "questions?" There is nothing worse than watching a speaker dribble out the words, "I guess if there are no questions, I should go. I guess I'm done. Goodbye." You cannot predict how good the audience questions will be (if there are any) or how good your answer will be. There are too many variables. Instead, write some strong closing remarks and memorize them. Deliver memorable visual or emotional images that will make your audience think. Be profound so they might be prompted to quote you later. Call them to action. Make them laugh. Show videotape. At the very least say, "Thank you for having me here." Whatever you do, make sure they know you are done. They will clap and you will be victorious.

IT'S ALWAYS ABOUT YOU:

Have you noticed that others around you are getting ahead because they speak better in public situations? Are YOU afraid to speak in front of large groups? What is it that makes you afraid? Possible failure? Looking stupid? Would it be more embarrassing to risk making a minor mistake than getting passed over for the next promotion you deserve? Force yourself to get up in front of people. If you don't want to speak in front of your coworkers, go to a Toastmasters Club or join a trade association to practice speaking in a safe, non-threatening environment. You'll be polishing your speaking skills on strangers who can't fire you. I'm telling you, this is the single most important work skill you can learn (outside of showing up every day). And keep this in mind. I promise that you will have no trouble speaking in public if you express your passions, your true point of view, or your best areas of expertise. Still don't think you can do it? Then, think how long you prattle on with total strangers about your wife, kids, and dog; without notes.

CHAPTER 22

WIN AWARDS

& GET FAMOUS.

Awards are another fast track way to getting noticed in your industry. When you can legally say you are an award winning...you name it...others will automatically trust your work. It's proof that you have excelled at something. Your peers will say, "He/she must be good. He/she won that big award." Open your newspaper and see how many movies advertise, "This movie features *Academy Award Winner*, Mel Gibson or Denzel Washington, or Jodie Foster. Gives the movie credibility, doesn't it? An award - ANY award in your industry gives you instant credibility. The very best kind of credibility are awards coming from your peers; people in your industry who are judging your work. *Not* your clients and customers.

The fact is that if your industry thinks you are the best, others will feel confident about hiring you to work for them.

How awesome is that?

So how do you go about winning one of those awards?

First, decide you are going to win. Research *how* those other folks won before you. What did they do? How did they attract attention? What did they do differently? I am the MC for a lot of corporate and association awards ceremonies, so I think I know. These winners delivered an outstanding achievement and/or performance. Often, they found an original point of view. A point of view that made their peers eyes bug out.

My friend, John Magnusson of the engineering firm; Skilling, Ward, Magnusson, & Barkshire in Seattle, Washington, makes it an annual mission to win awards. And they certainly do. His firm wins several state and national engineering awards, year after year, because he constantly sets the bar higher for his firm and his peers. They make it a goal to top every previous project. If you are ever in Seattle, visit the amazing *Experience Music Project* or the new *Seahawks Stadium*. They are two of John's recent national award winners that exemplify exactly what I'm talking about.

In other industries, award winners "decide" to sell more products or services than their associates do. Selling more than your peers always attracts attention.

You can even make huge strides in your career if you are "nominated" for an award. If you know the TV soap opera, *All My Children*, you know that Susan Lucci was nominated 19 times before she actually won the best actress award. She made a career out of being nominated. So if you get nominated, promote it. Talk about it. Post it on your stationary. Be proud of your achievement and jam it down your client's throat when you can.

You'll be rewarded with respect and advancement. You'll be offered more opportunities, more money, and more autonomy. And you'll deserve it because you are a celebrated leader in your industry. And remember, it's not you who is saying it, it's coming from your contemporaries.

As a guy who has (6) Emmys and (1) Iris on my office shelf, I can tell you those little statues have opened a lot of doors. I have made more cash and contacts because of my "credibility" than I ever would have as a non-award winning schlub. Why don't you give it a calculated shot? Aren't the award winners moving ahead of you? Why don't you unseat them? Or, at least make them nervous that you've entered the game.

IT'S ALWAYS ABOUT YOU:

Have you ever entered a corporate or association contest with the intention of winning? Why not? What do you have to lose? Why not enter and see where you "place." If you lose out, at least you'll see what it takes to win. Push yourself. Let people see the best work you've ever done. That is, unless you don't have the shelf space for awards.

CHAPTER 23

OBSESSED PEOPLE GET THINGS DONE.

Self-absorbed people are often told they are obsessed. I don't care. I'd still like to know them. I happen to love obsessed people. Obsessed people are able to make quantum leaps in their careers and they get things done!

The actor, Jim Carrey, is as obsessed off screen as the character he played in the movie, *Ace Ventura.* Obsession to his art is why he is able to cash his 20 million-dollar paychecks.

Jim was already a semi-famous comedian when I met him backstage at *The Punch Line* in Vancouver, British Columbia in 1987. He was in a dark corner adding more perfection to his impression of Henry Fonda and Sammy Davis Jr. Jim's impressions were already great. He didn't have to improve. Audiences screamed whenever he did these characters. But Jim was never satisfied. He knew there was an extra laugh in the body movement, the facial ticks, the voice, the language, and the attitude. And sure enough, his changes improved the performance that night by at least 20%.

Steve Oedekerk, who co-wrote *Ace Ventura*, with Jim, says the same thing. Steve recalled that Jim wanted to work long into most nights perfecting Ace's movements, his hand gestures, his stretched words, his...well...everything. So if you rent *Ace Ventura - Pet Detective*, you'll see that every one of Jim's (Ace's) words, phrases, physical nuances, and actions are mined for as much comic value as he could squeeze out of them. Truly a man obsessed with excellence.

Now, let me make the same observation about Steve Oedekerk, the writer of the first *Ace Ventura* film, and the writer/director of *Ace Ventura; When Nature Calls;* both worldwide box office hits.

Steve started out as an inventive stand up comedian and writer. He in fact, worked as a comedy writer for us during the Fox Late Show days. Aside from *Ace Ventura*, you know Steve as the screen writer of *Patch Adams, Nothing to Lose, Nutty Professor,* and *Jimmy Neutron, Boy Genius* (nominated for an Oscar), just to name a few. He is also in high demand as a film director, actor, and producer *(Nothing to Lose, Thumb Wars, "Thumbtanic, Kung Pow; Enter the Fist).*

Steve is a hot property because his films customarily surpass the coveted 100 million-dollar mark. The guy knows what to do on film to make people laugh and cry.

Steve's not lucky. He's disciplined, focused, and obsessed. He meticulously studies every detail of his work. The obsession started early with Steve. He's wanted to direct films ever since he was in High School. He's read libraries full of books on the subject. He's studied hundreds of movies to see how shots were done. And he's talked to everyone he could who had ever written a script or made a movie. He found out how much it would cost to make a movie and dutifully scrimped his pennies to make his first feature film; which cost him about $30,000. How did he save that much cash as a night club comic? Steve told me he figured out how to live on $1.00 a day; including rent and food. The rest went into his film fund. Can you imagine being so obsessed with dedication and sacrifice? Could you do that?

These days, Steve's frequent paychecks top $5,000,000. With his poorer days behind him, he has become quite extravagant. He thinks nothing of spending up to $2 bucks a day if he's feeling freaky. (He knows I'm kidding)

Yet another buddy of mine is comedian Kelly Monteith. Kelly is from St. Louis, Missouri and worked very hard to become a well-known comedian; which he did. You know Kelly from over 60 appearances on *The Tonight Show*, *David Letterman*, *Merv Griffin*, and the rest of the list is too long. Suffice it to say, he's on the short list of all time great ones. Kelly has had some major successes. (I think a couple of Command Performances for the Queen of England should count) But, like all of us, he has also suffered some major setbacks. Regardless, his character and integrity has always remained unfettered. So has his work ethic. He is obsessive about getting better every time he takes the stage.

As of this writing, the same healthy obsessive trait has found Kelly writing, producing, and directing his first motion picture. Here's where the marriage of integrity and obsession meet at the altar. Kelly has found a way to make a movie without any money! Everyone who knew anything about the film business said it absolutely couldn't be done. Kelly was smart <u>not</u> to listen to the experts. So committed was he to this project that he convinced everyone involved (camera, lights, actors, locations, etc.) to help out the film in return for payment when he sells it. That's guts, resourcefulness, obsession, and a strong will to do it his way and damn the movie studio system.

Now, here is my advice. Watch your local theater and buy a ticket when you see, *"A Lousy Ten Grand"* on the marquee. Kelly will thank you and so will the folks in the film who trusted an obsessed man.

IT'S ALWAYS ABOUT YOU:

What are you obsessed about? What do you think about 24/7? What would you sacrifice to make your obsession happen? If you can name it, then you are definitely obsessed. Channel that obsession in a productive way and go after it. Just be careful not to hurt others in your single-minded pursuit. Because if you step on people on the way up, you will see them again on the way down. That's obsession abuse and I will hunt you down and take this book away from you.

TURTLES CAN WIN, TOO.

Is being obsessed a little too aggressive for you? Not your style? Don't like to take big risks? Then relax. Go at your own pace. The slow, methodical route works, too.

Let me introduce you to a champion plodder; Jim Sharp.

Jim and I first met standing next to each other in line at our University of Puget Sound college graduation. Schrader, Shafer, Sharp, and so on. I found him to be instantly funny and easy to know. After graduation, Jim went on to teach 9th grade at Cedar Heights Junior High School in Port Orchard, Washington. We played on the same recreational league basketball team and drank a lot of beers.

After a few years of teaching, Jim came to me asking if I needed any help in my little advertising agency. He wanted a change and the comedy/media business appealed to his sense of humor. The timing was perfect. At the time, I was spending more of my time telling jokes on the road and the prospect of Jim taking over my advertising clients was serendipitous. So, I offered him a partnership. On his first day at the office he showed up with a rubber chicken; just to make sure he always "thought funny."

Our client stable was small; three carpet companies, a car dealership, and a small nursery. Jim's gentle sense of humor charmed his way into their hearts. What he didn't know about advertising he made up for with great customer service. His trick was just giving the clients exactly what they wanted. Plus, he was detailed, organized, creative and got the job done well, every time. As I got more notoriety as a comic, I got a few TV guest appearances. Eventually, I got an offer to create a local TV show of my own. Assembling a staff was easy. I didn't hesitate to make Jim my first "partner." That show, *Almost Live*, became a big Seattle success. Jim and I went on to collaborate on various TV shows from Vancouver, British Columbia to New York City to Los Angeles.

Throughout the years, Jim has been a steady plow horse. He doesn't take major risks and has continued to stay "on task" (his words). As a result, Jim has become a seasoned and respected specialist in every aspect of the television comedy business. He didn't branch off into game shows or "reality" shows. He's always loved comedy and stuck with it. He's also kept a list of everyone he's ever worked with. Networking mega-squared! And daddy, did it work! At this writing, Jim is the senior Vice President of the West Coast development office of Broadway Video - you know, the *Saturday Night Live* people! He's done numerous significant (meaning hideously expensive) network comedy and dramatic series and has developed an impeccable reputation in the television industry as a guy who can get things done.

Hold on, an important amendment.

I am adding a paragraph since the first draft. Jim got a big new job as a senior Vice President of Comedy Development at the Comedy Central Network. I don't know exactly how important his new job is. I just know that Jim's new house is a lot bigger.

Naturally, I had to give him a brand new rubber chicken for his office.

IT'S ALWAYS ABOUT YOU:

Are you more comfortable with taking a slower, steadier, less risky route? Take a lesson from Jim Sharp and stay "on task." Stay focused. Become a specialist and you will develop invaluable expertise in your field. Are you the best you can be in your field? Why not? What do you have to do to become the best? Don't let laziness creep in. Just 10% more effort yields a 50% gain. Doesn't sound possible? Ask any baseball player who bats 300. That's only hitting 3 out of every 10 pitches. Incidentally, Jim's other passion is baseball. No surprise, huh?

MAKE SURE YOUR PARADIGM SHIFT HAS A REVERSE GEAR.

In case you don't know this reference, a Paradigm Shift is a term popularized by trend watcher, Joel Barker. It refers to when the old rules/methods don't work anymore and a new rule/method becomes the new standard. "We made a major shift in our paradigm" is the kind of thing I often hear at sales celebration banquets. And they say it with some measure of relief in their voices. I guess too many top executives are afraid of getting caught behind the Paradigm Shift. Translation: Caught behind the current state of the art.

But change isn't always the answer. I think E-tailing was the last big one. If a company didn't spend silly money on web site development, security, and site maintenance they were destined to die an electronic death in the "new economy." Or so was the threat. Guess who died? The "new economy."

Ok, maybe I'm still bugged by the executives who want you to move your cheese. Or, those idiots who keep wanting you to "think out of the box." But even if I wasn't, I'd be crabby over any business who gets bullied by their competition into thinking THEY know something you don't; inciting you to question your business model and change your blessed paradigm. You know the one. The paradigm that put your company on the map in the first place! The box you are supposed to think out of is the same one that delivers your paycheck every week. It's a good box.

Joel Barker made a very successful series of videotapes giving examples of Paradigm Shifts. Like when the Swiss gave away 80% of their watch business to the Japanese by ignoring the upstart quartz battery revolution. *That* was a true Paradigm Shift in the way watches were produced and sold.

The same could be said for the move from steam power to internal combustion engines. But folks, those shifts didn't sneak up on anybody. Everyone had plenty of time to test the shift before retooling. The more important question is WHY do we have to shift the paradigm? Now, I'm all in favor of repackaging your products so they will fit into my computer bag or glove compartment. Tiny bags of potato chips, Keebler cookies, and travel Excedrin make perfect sense. But drastic changes disturb profit. For example, why does the giant Coca Cola Company keep trying to put itself out of business? New Coke was a colossal disaster. Luckily, somebody kept a copy of the old recipe and threw the paradigm shifter into reverse. But now they have introduced New Coke with Lemon? Here is my letter to them. "Dear Coca Cola, you don't need to flavor your cola with lemon. You have been tricked. People like me put a slice of lemon in your major competitor, Pepsi, to make Pepsi taste more like Diet Coke! Did someone "at corporate" respond to a Pepsi practical joke memo?! Or, did you get your hands on a tainted corporate espionage document? PS: What's the deal with Vanilla Coke?"

And, what about *The Today Show* host, Matt Lauer's new hairstyle? I liked the OLD hairstyle, didn't you? The adult one. Not the spiky, distracting buzz cut. Matt, I've worked alongside you. You are a very handsome man but now you look like Sting-turned-network anchor. Please don't confess to me that you're also wearing bowling shoes as a fashion statement?

Oh, you can attempt to make the argument that the pop singer, Madonna, goes through a paradigm shift every other year with her hair and wardrobe; but you'd be wrong. She still sounds just like Madonna when you slip one of her CD's into your car stereo. She doesn't change her "sound" for change sake. Like Frito Lay, she just repackages what she already owns.

It's so hard to get something right...a product, a service, an image, or whatever, that captures the public's fancy so perfectly that people line up by the thousands to buy it, watch it, or use it. A hit is nearly impossible to find. So if you ever stumble upon one, leave it alone until the public demands a change.

Shifting the paradigm just to be progressive is expensive and foolish.

As for responding to the competition's paradigm shift, let THEM make the mistakes. Let THEM sink millions into research and development while you rack up your tidy perennial profit. If you are losing market share, look for weakness in your customer service department, your order fulfillment department, and your sales team; before you flush your system down the toilet in search of a brand new failure.

A few years ago, I hosted a TV show and our ratings were awful. It puzzled everyone but me. It was a sketch comedy show that needed guest stars to participate. Except that no guests would come on the show. Problematic even to the civilian viewer, wouldn't you say? Bottom line was that we couldn't afford to get great comedy writers. And because we had marginal writing, good guests wouldn't risk looking stupid on our show. Would you?

The "experts" at the network thought a Paradigm Shift would rescue the show.

The producers announced the following solution to the staff. "We are going to put Ross in sweaters! And we're going to change the set to make it look more casual. That will surely be more inviting to the guests."

Guess what happened?

The writing was still bad even though I was in comfortable sweaters. The set was cozy...and empty. Predictably, our cancellation soon followed. I'm sure there were conferences at the network like, "If only we could have addressed Ross' wardrobe sooner." CBS did the same thing with Pat Sajak when he had his late night talk show. I watched him go from a suit and desk (ala Jay Leno & Dave Letterman) to a cushy couch and (you guessed it) really nice sweaters. That's when I knew he was headed for the late night bone pile.

Don't fall for the Paradigm Shift ploy unless you are still riding to work in a horse and buggy. Oops, did I just accidentally insult our Amish readers? Then, I retract that statement. I love the Jayco travel trailers you build and your furniture is utterly amazing! (Writing a book in a sensitive politically correct environment is hard. I can't believe I just sucked up to the Amish)

IT'S ALWAYS ABOUT YOU:

What shifts are taking place in your industry? What do you think about the changes? Are they necessary? Can you reverse them if you have to? Are shifts being made out of fear from the competition? Or are the shifts truly the way of the future. Why not question the obvious and risk nothing? After all, it's not like you are the Ford Motor Company having to recall the Explorer.

FOR

MANAGERS

&

OTHER

KNOW-IT-ALLS

CHAPTER 26

STOP IDOLIZING JACK WELCH.

If you are a manager, you have probably been instructed to read about this guy. Frankly, I am so frigging tired of books hailing the former CEO of General Electric as the corporate leader of the century. How many books have been written about him?

Lots.

How many are best sellers?

Most.

I see these books on airplanes, conference tables and desks everywhere I go. Ok, I've even read a couple. But I don't understand the Jack Welch fever. Sure, he grew his company. But when he took over GE in 1981, he had 400,000 employees, 25 billion in annual revenue, banks full of cash, and some battle tested mangers. Talk about a head start!

Jack's success reminds me of that old joke, "How do you make two million dollars? Well, first you start with a million dollars, then all you do is...." Yeah, right. What about that backbreaking first million? Is Jack Welch higher on the genius ladder than men like Sam Walton, Warren Buffet or Bill Gates? I've met all of these guys and none of them walk on water. They make mistakes and have insecurities; just like you and me. At least Sam, Warren and Bill started from ground zero. They believed in their own ideas and carefully orchestrated themselves into billionaires. No head starts.

Jack had other advantages. He graduated from the University of Illinois with a Ph.D. in engineering. Which of us had the option to stay in school *that* long? Consequently, Jack had his pick of some of the top entry-level positions in the country. Not that he didn't work hard, but his business career has been blessed ever since he donned a cap and gown.

A Friendly Reminder: Jack isn't You.

Even as a young manager, Jack played with big marbles. He was able to pour hundreds of thousands of dollars into a sinking operation to save it. For giggles, Jack would go in and do a "deep dive," as he called it, where he would invest a lot of time, energy and cash into an underachieving company like CNBC to re-energize it. Which one of us works for a company that has that sort of surplus bankroll? He also had the human resources to scour his company for the top talent and give them mind-boggling incentives to step in and turn around the ailing divisions. Which of us could cherry-pick from a 400,000+ talent pool? I'm telling you, Noah's ark wouldn't have sunk if Noah had a blank check and his choice of several factory built vessels.

Nobody Moved Your Cheese!

Let's not forget that Jack also had some very big and expensive failures along the journey. How about the time his team literally blew the roof off of a GE plastics chemical plant; with its various and sundry dangers. That goof didn't even earn a wrist slapping by the boss. Or, the major slip up Jack suffered (albeit, not personally) when he bought his way into the investment banking biz; acquiring Kidder-Peabody. A faux pas that cost "his" GE 400 million dollars - and he got to keep his job?! Hell, I'd bet even Sam Walton would fire himself for such a colossal blunder. I mean, could you or me blow 1/10,000th of that much dough and still collect a check on the 1st and 15th? Jack got a free pass on these mistakes because (1) his company didn't have anyone better to lead the troops and (2) GE had pockets so deep, you could see the rings of Saturn on the other side.

So, back to my original question. Why is Jack Welch considered such a corporate darling? I think it's because so many middle managers in corporate America see his path as accessible to them. In one sense I can see their point. Jack Welch is proof that if you stick with it for thirty + years, enough people will quit or screw up so that you can win by default. But look behind the curtain and you'll see that Jack Welch's success was in being able to publicly celebrate his victories, privately downplay his disasters, and consistently finesse his way to the top. Well done, Jack. You got out alive. And all kidding aside, you actually changed the world in some ways. But forgive us if we don't herald you as the Second Coming of Adam Smith.

Plus, Adam Smith didn't know about perks. Now that Jack is getting divorced we can pick up a newspaper and see the lifelong corporate perks Jack is entitled to; like meals, private planes, free apartment rental, and so on. Some of you may think I am kicking the man whiles he's down. Consider this. If you are a GE stockholder those perks are coming out of your pocket and into the pants of a guy worth almost a billion dollars. And to think that you and I still have to buy our own meals. Absurd.

Hey! Hey! Who turned out the lights?

IT'S ALWAYS ABOUT YOU:

What business gods have you been worshiping? What gurus have you patterned your life after? Do they really strike such a perfect parallel with your life?

Why are they any better than you? Why can't you carve out your own path? The answer is that you can. Go ahead and admire Sam Walton, Bill Gates, or Jack Welch.

Borrow some of the specific tricks of their trade. But don't put them on an impossible pedestal. Nobody has a life exactly like yours. In fact, duplicating someone else's life is an attempt to become a faded photocopy - never as crisp and clear as the original.

The better journey is to think that someday, someone will be writing a book about YOUR life.

CHAPTER 27

THROW OUT YOUR BUSINESS PLAN.

Recently, I was asked to be the Master of Ceremonies for a park dedication. Exciting life I lead, huh? I wondered. "How can I make dedicating trees and shrubs funny?"

It turned out to be a hoot. My job was to write a "semi-roast" around the park's benefactor; a University of California at Santa Barbara professor/scientist/multi-millionaire named, Dr. Virgil Elings. Virgil saved this park when he donated four million dollars.

How does a college professor dig up 4 mil? Virgil is an inventor who holds 54 patents and has created such things as a device to measure lung water. His company, Digital Instruments, was a world-beater in the atomic microscope sector. So much so, that Virgil's $50,000 original investment turned into a $250 million sale when he turned in the keys in 1999.

From his reputation, I expected to meet an eccentric scientist and engineer. He wasn't. He was a blast. What really tickled me about Virgil is that he treated me to some of the wisest contrarian business insight I'd ever heard. Virgil said, "If I've had any success it's because I threw out my business plans and just concentrated on making the best damn products in the world." (FYI: I inserted the word "damn" to replace his far more colorful adjective)

Virgil is convinced the reason so many companies fail is that teams of high level "managers" spend days, months, even years devising a business plan and then do everything possible to stick to it; including riding that business plan into bankruptcy.

Maybe you've been involved in a plan to generate more market share or force a product down your customer's throat; only to have it soundly rejected. Dr. Elings' singular notion is that, "Nobody knows if the plan will work. The plan is always changing because we are always uncovering new information. At Digital Instruments, our "plan" was to make a million dollars and we couldn't have failed more miserably!" (His company made over 100+ million a year profit).

Virgil was also criticized for buying a defunct clothing "outlet center" in Solvang, Calif. His close friends said, "Virgil, why did you buy that vacant building complex? What do you plan to do with it?" Virgil's reply was, "Gee, I just bought a building and land for 25% of what it cost to build it. And I bought it in one of the fastest growing areas of Southern California. I guess while I watch the property value go up I'll store my motorcycles in there." (Virgil owns about 100 vintage motorcycles and has created a profitable museum out of his vacant outlet center.)

Think of it. Intel's original plan was to make memory chips but they couldn't do it as well as other companies so they switched to making computer processors.

Bill Gates' plan was not to sell operating systems. But that's what IBM thought he was selling. So, he went out to find one he could peddle.

The wonder drug, Viagra, was originally supposed to be a compound to treat hypertension (high blood pressure). Turned out that something else got tense.

I never planned to be the host of a daily radio show or a TV Game Show. I never even considered them as a possibility. But when the offers came in, the money was so good and I had so much fun, I couldn't refuse.

These are all carefully designed master "plans" that changed when the circumstances changed.

IT'S ALWAYS ABOUT YOU:

What plan have you concocted lately? Are you willing to throw it all away if it doesn't work? Or, are you going to make it work no matter what? Maybe you are afraid that if it doesn't work you'll look like a failure? Well, if you stay "married" to the plan and it ends up costing the firm a lot more money, won't you look even dumber? Why not keep an open mind. Maybe you'll have success with an outgrowth of the plan? Who knows, you might unwittingly uncover the next Viagra. (If you do, call me. I'd like to invest)

CHAPTER 28

GOOD CUSTOMER SERVICE CAN BANKRUPT YOU.

I have a personal vendetta against horrible customer service. Drives me crazy. So crazy that five of the HR training films I've produced have been about customer service. And with as much as I've learned, I am still convinced you can go out of business with good customer service.

How can that be?

Because good customer service isn't good enough anymore. Today, it takes *unforgettable* Customer Service to win big! Customer Service of mythic proportions will bring people back. Sounds like a lot of work, doesn't it? It is. Competition is so fierce and dollars are so scarce that your customers must have such an extraordinary experience that *they'd* consider themselves insane to buy from anyone else. Better yet, they would tell their friends in the process.

Mind you, I grew up with Nordstrom in my back yard. So, I was used to exceptional customer service. In fact, as a smart-ass teenager, I used to return all kinds of crap just to see if they would take it back. The boldest I ever got with Nordstrom was after a family reunion. I took back a 20-cup coffee maker. (Nordstrom is a clothing store. They don't sell coffee makers.) When I was asked to fill out the "reason for return form," I wrote, "worked great, just needed it for the party." I got a full refund without a receipt. And yes, my Mom made me give it back.

There are a lot of funny people in my trade. So, I am acutely aware that if I don't give my customers *more* than what they expect, in my case laughs, they won't come back. And brother, I need them to come back. I need them to tell their friends and family I am funny so they'll buy tickets the next time I am in town. These laughers are my customer base. And I want them to be happy. I even have a no-bombing policy, which means I'll give you a full refund if you don't think I delivered the laughs you were expecting. Knock on wood, I have never had to pay back a dime.

And to think I learned it best from a room service waitress (for security purposes) I'll call, Maria Garcia.

I was in Orlando, Florida entertaining for a Burroughs office equipment conference. I checked into the Orlando Marriott Hotel; absolutely starving. I called room service and ordered a cheeseburger and a Diet Coke. When the room service waitress rang my doorbell, she brought in a mouth-watering, mile high cheeseburger and a Diet Pepsi. She said they didn't have any more Diet Coke in the kitchen and hoped the Pepsi would be OK. I was polite but told her I was "Jones-ing" for a Diet Coke and asked her to please take the Pepsi back.

She left.

Forty seconds later, my doorbell rang again and the same server is standing there with an ice cold Diet Coke. I said, "I thought you said the kitchen was out of Coke?" She replied, "We are. But I got this one out of the machine two floors down." I tried to pay her but she wouldn't take my money. She said, "I just want you to be happy at our hotel."

When I regained consciousness, I jumped to the phone to ring the hotel manager. I rattled on and on; bragging about this woman. Then, I asked him for the Marriott International headquarters so I could continue my crusade about this lady. My cheeseburger got cold, the home fries got rigor mortis - and I didn't even care!

That was customer service of mythic proportions! For the dollar she spent on that Diet Coke, the Marriott won a lifetime customer.

What happened to Maria Garcia? I called a couple of years later and found out she had been named the food & beverage manager at one of their Boston properties. Gee, what a surprise.

Who says exceptional customer service goes unnoticed. That particular act of great customer service was noticed by a guy (me) who was in a position to talk about it in public; over and over again. By now, I'll bet 100,000 people have heard about Maria Garcia. YOU make it 100,001. I even put her story in a training film that we sell all around the world.

Now, I'm going to scare you into being a monument of grand customer service. In November of 2002 in Van Nuys, California, a man got into an argument with an auto parts clerk over some brake pads. The clerk didn't satisfy the customer so the customer got mad and left. A little later the angry customer came back to the store. This time he didn't have the brake shoes. He had a gun and he shot the clerk. The ultimate refund.

You never know who is paying attention to your treatment of them. Or, what kind of a mood that person is in when you meet them. I do know one thing. If you deliver customer service of mythic proportions you'll have an easy shortcut to success.

Pull a "Maria Garcia" and see who notices YOU. See who helps get YOU promoted.

IT'S ALWAYS ABOUT YOU:

Is your customer service the stuff of legends? Why not? Are you the kind of person who only offers the bare minimum? What could you do that would blow your clients and customers away? Can you remember the last time you were amazed? Did you tell anybody about it? Try doing something amazing yourself. Then, stand back and watch the magic happen to your career.

CHAPTER 29

CONSULTANTS

ARE SCAMS.

Anybody can be a consultant. Including you. There are no tests to take, no board requirements, and no diploma to qualify you to be a consultant. You don't have to even be that successful. C'mon, that's a great scam.

For many years, there was a guy named, Howard Shenson, who toured the United States giving seminars on how to be a consultant. I went to one. I don't know if he ever really consulted anybody or if he just taught seminars. But Howard was very convincing. At least he was convincing to the 40 or 50 of us who were looking for a way to translate our experiences into ready cash.

From what I remember, Howard told us that all we needed were balls big enough to call ourselves a "consultant" and some quickie business cards. And, BAM! You're in business.

It's a simple scam for you, the consultant, and a cheap scam for the company that hires you. You get a higher hourly wage than you ever earned when you were employed (maybe even by the same company.) The company gets specialized on-staff skills without having to kick in for a 401K, health insurance, or a severance package. Everybody wins, right?

I'm sure you've seen consultants snooping around your company. They come in half days or a few days a month and allegedly bring some outside expertise and/or an outsider's perspective. It's a sweet job that lives up to its billing.

I've done it myself, many times, and I love doing it.
I've been a comedy writing consultant for software companies who wanted to punch up their owner's manuals.

I've been a comedy consultant for TV production companies who want to inject a veteran into a room of newcomers.

I've been a public speaking coach to top executives and athletes who want "tips and tricks of the speaking trade."

And, I've been a marketing consultant to companies who need an infusion of fresh and original ideas.

How much would I charge? Usually, I'd start at $2,500/day and see if they threw up. If they did, I would give them a half-day rate of $1,500.

How did I come up with those figures?

At first, I didn't know how much to charge so I made up a figure. Then, I found out that's pretty close to what the top people earn.

Expensive? Sure it is. But would you hire a consultant for $75 bucks a day? Nope! You would assume he/she wasn't worth a damn. Perception is invaluable.

But consider this.

To make this scam pay off, you need to be able to deliver the goods. Yes, you actually have to *earn* the money.

My buddy, John Lloyd, has the perfect consultant model. John worked for a huge pharmaceutical company for almost twenty years. John is brilliantly detailed and a great sales motivator. But he got tired of criss-crossing the planet and wanted to work from home while his baby daughter was growing up. So, John quit. On his way out, he made an attractive deal with his former company to provide valuable research consulting services he knew they needed.

They bit.

John had his first client.

One client is all you need to be a successful consultant because you can use that client as a reference for others.

Within two years John was making four times what he ever made as an employee. And, he never had to leave his house.

It doesn't matter what skills you have. There are consultants in every imaginable field. And, since so many companies are "right sizing," they'll hire a consultant part time instead of keeping a full timer on the payroll.

As much teasing as I have done about consultants being scams, their pinpointed expertise can offer a quick and timely remedy; even for you.

When I was first starting out, I kidded a fellow comedian (Bill Nye) that I would get ahead faster if I could hire a comedy consultant. He told me that one actually existed. In the tiny Sonoma Valley town of Sebastopol, California there was the comedy coach I mentioned earlier named, Jim Richardson. He taught a comedy class at a local college and in his spare time coached up and coming comedians. I emptied my savings and drove from Seattle to Northern California to meet him.

He said he would work with me at a rate of something like $200/hour. A fortune to me, at the time. But for that fee, he analyzed my act, edited me, and encouraged me to perfect all forms of comedy; one-liners, stories, physical humor, audience participation, sight gags - the works. Was it a scam? Sure it was. But, thanks to his coaching, I won the Seattle International Comedy Competition; which indeed propelled my career to the level of Headliner.

It was quite a scam for Jim Richardson, too. He got a no-name comic to fork over $200 bucks an hour. I'm pretty sure he just made up that figure.

IT'S ALWAYS ABOUT YOU:

If you are hiring consultants, are you getting your moneysworth? Are they overcharging you? Could someone on your staff perform the same duty? Could a friend of yours come in for a few days and give you an outsider's view, for free? What about your board members? Can't they drop by more often? Isn't their seasoned advice what you pay them for?

Or, could You be a consultant? Take an inventory of your skills and make a list of clients who might buy your services. Check the Internet and see what a person like you charges for that service. This is the lowest capital expenditure business you can start. If you believe in your abilities, you can do it from your home; without an assistant. Print some business cards and stationary with your Microsoft Publisher program and you can get in on this scam just like the rest of us.

CHAPTER 30

MANAGEMENT RETREATS CAN KILL MORALE.

As a comedian and MC, I've participated in about a hundred and fifty management retreats over the years. My job was to "glue it all together" or provide "after dinner entertainment" following a hard day of...retreating. I am grateful to all of the companies who have hired me.

But sadly, most of these retreats backfired and damaged employee morale. Only a few ever succeeded to improve performance and motivate people to be their best. I'll talk about (1) the disastrous ones, (2) the best retreat model I've ever seen and (3) what to do if you get invited to one.

I don't fault management, entirely. I'd rather point the finger of blame at the professional meeting moderators who sold management on the idea of a closed-door retreat in the first place.

I'm sure the idea sounded good, at first. Top management would go away for a weekend, get everyone together, and learn some new things about their company. Or better yet, galvanize team spirit. The "professional moderator" then shows up to encourage all of the team members to "open up" and spill their guts to the brass about what serious company problems need to be addressed. Employees are told that this is a "safe environment" and are encouraged to speak freely. Some even say, "Don't worry. Everything said in this room stays in this room." Meanwhile, a rogue camera crew is videotaping the whole event. How secret is that? The tension is as thick and sticky as mid-summer Texas asphalt.

With this open mouth policy, management can't help but notice potential troublemakers and those irritating speaker-uppers. (I always wonder how much of that free speech ends up in a performance review.) I'll bet that when the company reconvenes back home, there is a lot of lunchroom chatter like, "Can you believe what Sandy said at the retreat? I think she's burnt her stew for the last time."

Besides that, management doesn't hear what they want to hear. They want real solutions to improve profitability. Instead, the meetings get bogged down with complaints like bad parking spaces, terrible air conditioning, a quirky computer system, a laughable ad campaign, not enough sales brochures, too many back orders, sloppy warehouse personnel, and a dyslexic receptionist who transposes client phone numbers.

No surprise they need a comedian to inject some comic relief. I've probably saved a lot of execs from cardiac arrest.

Now, for the good one.

The best retreat I've ever witnessed was a 3-day retreat I hosted for Motorola. Specifically the IDEN group that makes the phones used by Nextel. The host hotel was *The Breakers* in West Palm Beach, Florida. *The Breakers* is 100 years old, stuffy and famously formal. But this group stripped an elegant meeting room of all its pomposity and transformed it into an intimate and comfortable space. The production group filled the room with leather loveseats, a red velvet sexy speaker's couch, and no podium. The walls were covered in muslin and served as backdrops for projected music videos and tie-died lighting. This was not your Daddy's Motorola. This was Motorola Unplugged.

To set the stage for you, this is a division of Motorola that has been enormously profitable, even in a bad economy. This retreat was testimony to the fact that the IDEN Group was willing to spend a lot of money to keep their people on top.

The Motorola executives didn't expect the employees to "open up" and slog the meeting with solutions or gripes. Instead, they brought in an extremely diverse group of top-notch speakers who represented the state of the art in technology, trends, music, fashion, behavioral economics, sports, management, and even the treatment of animal testing. I mean, we sat in this room with people as diverse as rap producer, Russell Simmons, to MIT professor, Dr. Dan Ariely, to football Hall of Famer, Terry Bradshaw. Motorola was even bold enough to fly in two technical writers from England who had lambasted Motorola products in their magazine, T-3 (Tomorrow's Technology Today). How often does a company subject itself to criticism, on purpose?

It was my job to keep things light and provide a fun segue between speakers.

The attendees had a blast!

I had the time of my life!

The retreat was fun, insightful, shocking, and informative. I know these people left stimulated and ready to tackle the year. They were definitely armed with the ammunition to make more money for themselves and their company.

I wanted to fill out an application myself!

IT'S ALWAYS ABOUT YOU:

So, what can *You* do if you are invited to attend one of these potentially hazardous retreat adventures? Since this is about You and Your future, sit back and listen carefully. What are people REALLY talking about? What does management REALLY want to take home from this retreat? Should you participate in the "opening up" part? Sure, but confine your comments to systems NOT personnel. Concentrate on solutions not bitching. Finally, less talk is more in these situations. No need to shoot yourself unnecessarily if you don't have to.

It reminds me of that old story about the Billionaire and his wife who go to a fancy cocktail party at a friend's mansion. Everyone at the party is bragging about their vacations, their political opinions, and their latest corporate successes; everyone <u>except</u> the Billionaire. He just smiles and listens. He doesn't even interrupt when he knows someone is wrong. In the car on the way home, his wife is livid, "Why didn't you jump in and argue with Niles when you knew he was an idiot?" The Billionaire said, "I already know what I think, I wanted to find out what he thought."

If you are lucky enough to find yourself in a more relaxed learning environment like the Motorola retreat, soak up as much as you can from the expensive experts. Then, compare their perspective with your specific real world experiences.

Finally, be thankful their fees didn't come out of your pocket.

CHAPTER 31

DON'T LISTEN TO THOSE FEAR MONGERING FUTURISTS.

Futurists are a fairly new phenomenon and I don't like them. One step below telephone psychic, Miss Cleo.

I meet my share of futurists because I am usually on the speaking bill with them. I think it's a meeting planner's rule. Fun always follows terror.

Look, I'm sure these futurist people are smart. Their credentials usually contain a Ph.D. in math or engineering from a respected university. They also seem to be without any identifiable personality or sense of humor. Yet they, not so philanthropically, squeeze a $25-40,000/hour speaking fee out of a willing company in exchange for tendering their "research."

If you are the company who hired him/her, what do you get for your money? A droll hour of slides or a Power Point presentation designed to send shock waves through the audience. Academics telling pragmatists the future of their business.

I witnessed one of these soothsayers at a huge Telecommunications conference where he told the congregation of phone company owners that their copper wired phone lines would be extinct by the year 2015; replaced with fiber optic cable. Their 300 billion dollars in capital equipment would only be worth 5 billion, by that time. Further, that these independent phone companies would be out of business if they didn't "go wireless" right away. He went on to say that they should throw all of their money into broad band "big pipes" if they wanted to stay alive. How does he know? It can't be from empirical data because that's a collection of past outcomes. Future outcomes are derived from extrapolation and forecasting.

We're talking about educated guesses, at best. It's like the old "rumors become fact" syndrome; where enough people panic in response to the rumor that it soon becomes a fact.

Recently, we have been hearing real estate futurists predict that the rapidly rising home prices will result in a "bubble" that will burst like the Internet bubble. And how is the market responding to this news? Already, housing starts are slowing. People are bailing out of their homes with the hope of snagging a profit before the bottom drops out. And the instant interest rates swing up, the bubble will surely burst. But more from pre-conditioning or true valuation?

Futurists can't predict the future. But I think they can *create* the future by scaring people into action. I wondered if the owners of these companies went home, divested and made his future come true out of fear?

So, the next time you hear a "Futurist" predict the course of your life, question what he/she says. Don't take their interpolated "data" at face value because data can be manipulated to make any point.

Just to be sure, I checked. The future isn't here yet.

IT'S ALWAYS ABOUT YOU:

Who are you listening to for advice, these days? Who do you get your answers from about your job future? Your relationship future? The future of the world? Do these people really know what they are talking about or are they making totally unfounded predictions to make a name for themselves? Future forecasting is akin to rumor mongering. Beware of spreading rumors. When a believable rumor circulates it can affect people's behavior. Rumors can become truth if they get enough support.

Example: If you heard a rumor that your company was going to be bought out, you might start weighing your other options - looking for other work - maybe even get another offer. But since you can't trust rumors and you can't foresee the future, take your lessons from the past. Try not to repeat the same mistakes and worry about the future when it gets here.

CHAPTER 32

THE STOCK MARKET IS RIGGED.

Aw man, I wrote this chapter six months before we knew about the fall of Enron and WorldCom. Regardless, you got the message. Big companies can easily manipulate their stock price and lure you into investing. They can shift losses to different quarters. They can move acquisitions to other divisions to boost profits. Or, they can move tons of excess cash in and out of foreign currency to take advantage of the tax laws. And you didn't have a vote in any of that. You just bought the stock from your broker or over the Internet hoping to double your money; never knowing really why it went up or down.

Then there are the stock analysts who can get TV airtime to tout their favorites, drive the price up, and unload them for an inflated profit. "Pump and Dump," it's called.

Ross Shafer 187

I used to trade stocks online and I would see one of the major brokerage firms on TV saying, "We are staying with XYZ Company. We own it and we are not selling." Liar! I subscribed to Level Two streaming real-time stock quotes and I could see the actual sales on my computer. The same company would be selling shares of XYZ; *WHILE THE ANALYST WAS ON TV* bragging about keeping it in their portfolio!

Fortunately, some of these financial media manipulators are being whisked off to jail. Unfortunately, it's too late for the thousands of employees who lost their retirement money; all of it.

Oh yes, and then there are those badly managed companies who simply go out of business while telling their employees things are going to turn around, "as soon as we do some restructuring." Consolidated Freightways, the giant trucking firm who had been in business for 75 years filed for bankruptcy and 19,000 of their employees hit the street. Their money gone. However, what would you bet the principles saw it coming and took their money out before the fall.

Investing in a company you aren't running is a huge risk to your IRA and your family. Take a look at your business card. Unless you are you the CEO, CFO, COO, President, or have privileged access to the inner financial circle of your company, stay away from their stock. Oh, I know that won't be popular with your company because they gave you stock options and a great strike price, right? They might even be matching your stock contributions. Hmm...sounds enticing but remember, there is no guarantee the company you work for will make the best decisions about your future. That goes for the managers of your retirement fund, too. They could make a few bad investments, with your money, and poof! You're broke and you had nothing to do with it because you weren't allowed to see the crash coming.

So what do you do with your excess cash? You can let it sit in a low interest bank account or you can do something totally wild; invest in yourself. With very little money, you can start a side business you might actually love. Turn your avocation into profit. Success is easy when you are doing something you're excited about.

Do you like gardening? Buy garden tools or a tractor and do it for other people. Do you like dogs? Breed them. Train them. Invest in a kennel and board them for. Can you build web sites? Buy a computer and some programs and charge money for your expertise. Every time I have tried to make money or invest in some venture I didn't know anything about (see Pet Shop), my money didn't know what it was doing either and I lost a ton. Stick with what you know and you'll stay in control of your money. What's better than being the President of your own investment?

IT'S ALWAYS ABOUT YOU:

Where else could you put your excess money? What business have you always wanted to start out of your garage? What stopped you? Do you believe in yourself more than a phantom manager at a company you don't work for? Why not? You work hard for your money. Why not invest in yourself? After all, aren't you the world's greatest expert on YOU?

CHAPTER 33

I HOPE YOU

GO BROKE.

I just reread the last chapter and laughed. You won't listen to me. You will think what I said doesn't apply to you and you will invest in the stock market. In which case, good luck. But I hope you go broke. It will be good for you. Nobody talks about the benefits of going broke. I've been broke a few times and it's been the greatest pain I've ever suffered through. I sure hope you get the chance.

Until you are desperately scrambling to make ends meet, you don't know squat about the sweet value of success. Until you are calling creditors to "make arrangements" or kiting checks, stalling payments, or otherwise living paycheck to scarce paycheck, you won't know how to keep getting off the floor when the tough times knock you down. And brother, you *will* get knocked down.

Tough times hit everybody. Truly successful people expect it but keep getting out of bed. I have undying respect for anybody who has survived and thrived after having been wiped out by illness, divorce, or other natural disasters. When you are wading waist deep in dept, you find out quickly if you have the will and resourcefulness to overcome it. Or, you'll find out if you feel victimized; frozen by fear. Which kind of person are you? The kind of person who will persevere and win...or the kind who will trade in your dignity for a cardboard sign on the side of the road?

I've come dangerously close to the cardboard sign, myself.

After I had paid my dues and worked myself up the broadcast ladder, hosted a couple of network TV shows - and made a lot of money, I hit a serious dead spell. My Big Time game show was cancelled. This was my third cancellation in three years. My career was definitely cooling off.

We had a big beautiful home with a big beautiful mortgage and a tragically stereotypical television personality's lifestyle. Without a steady income, the cruise ship-size anchor of debt was dragging us under. Steadily, we depleted our savings by making payments to our creditors. We soon lost our house to foreclosure. My non-working wife left me. I tried everything I could think of to make ends meet. The comedy club business had slowed down and I was only working a few days a month. And, since I had spent the last eight years in broadcasting, no advertising agency would touch me without a current resume in that field. (I didn't have a plan "B" at this point)

I finally took a job selling infomercial TV time on a local Los Angeles cable station. It was my job to walk into Doctor and

Dentist offices in an effort to sell them on the idea of making their own infomercial.

It was humiliating.

They would look at me and say, "Hey! Weren't you the guy on TV? What the hell are you doing here? Is your career that far in the toilet?"

Yes, it was. But I didn't quit.

I took every odd job that came along. I even painted houses for awhile. Due to my skill level, most of them had to be repainted.

After an incredibly humbling few years, I got back into broadcasting with a modest but steady paycheck. This time I did it *without* the celebrity lifestyle and expenses to match.

I worked nights and weekends creating a corporate speaking career, an HR Video Training company and a consulting practice standing at the ready for when the TV job would eventually be cancelled (which it was) Now, I have plan "B" - "C" - and "D" thankfully supporting me. Whew!

The truly successful people I've met don't take failure personally. Maybe the circumstances had nothing to do with you. You just got caught in the back draft. Or maybe it was your fault by making an error in judgement. Who hasn't screwed up? Get over it and move on. If your bills are too high, cut your expenses. Move out of your expensive home and get a smaller place. Turn in your leased vehicle or sell something valuable and regroup. Yes, it hurts to give up your "luxuries" but successful people know that the bad times are only temporary. Good times will come back.

How often have you heard someone say, "That guy made and lost several fortunes." The key word is "several." He/she has made fortunes several times. That's ignoring failure in search of the next success.

Want more examples? Larry King, the broadcaster, went bankrupt in the 60's. He's worth millions today. Muhammad Ali was rich, famous and then went dead broke before he fought Joe Frazier. Ali came back bigger and more famous than ever before. They both had the fortitude (I was going to say balls but you might be a woman) to come back. They never stopped believing in themselves and their talent; even when people close to them had lost faith.

IT'S ALWAYS ABOUT YOU:

Have you ever been broke? How did you handle it? Were you a victim? Or were you dedicated to getting up every day and looking for work? Did you file bankruptcy or did you pay off your creditors? If you ever went broke, could you swallow your pride and take a job you would normally think was beneath you? These are questions that should challenge your character. Did you pass the test?

Actor John Ritter says his life is like a mountain – lots of peaks and valleys. And you never know which one is waiting over the next hill.

My father used to tell my brothers and me, "Life goes in cycles." Sometimes you'll be up. Sometimes you'll be down. But don't let your pride destroy you. Sweep a parking lot or dig a ditch. It will put food on your table and strengthen your back bone."

ADMIT IT.

YOU

AIN'T

PERFECT.

CHAPTER 34

EVERYBODY IS SCREWED UP... NOT JUST YOU.

Do you question your decisions? Do you feel like you are in over your head; unable to do the job you are being asked to do?

My guess is you're probably right.

That's OK. Everybody gets just as screwed up as you are.

It doesn't matter how old you are, how successful you are, or how experienced you happen to be, everybody gets scared. I've experienced those attitudes in my executive speech coaching sessions. But when you think about it, why wouldn't top executives be scared? Everyone has insecurities and scars from their life experiences.

If you watch the daytime talk shows, you'll see that we all have social and cultural reasons to be screwed up.

We come from single parent homes. We are dyslexic. We have Attention Deficit Disorder. We have Post Traumatic Stress Syndrome. We were sexually abused. We didn't get enough hugs as children. We got TOO MUCH love as children. We've witnessed a suicide. We've had our hearts trounced on by ex-spouses. We were beaten up by bullies. We have too much debt. We lost somebody in the war. We grew up rich and sheltered. We grew up poor and joined a gang. We've used too many drugs. We have a hidden addiction. Our religion won't permit it. We have an eating disorder. And worst of all, Jerry Springer will let us talk about it on national TV.

Since these are the same people who run organizations, it's no wonder so many companies are in a fragile state of flux. No wonder so many of them fail.

But that's the curse of being human. Everybody feels unsure about major decisions, from time to time. Even you.

Don't feel bad about it. Admit you're not perfect.

The stakes are high. Running any operation is loaded with stress. Being responsible for the livelihoods of your employees or subordinates can easily fill your nights with bad dreams. Not to mention, in a climate of rampant mergers and acquisitions, odds are pretty good that you will be promoted to a job you aren't qualified to do. Your boss retired, was laid off, or downsized and you're the only one left. So what if you don't deserve to be the manager? Deal with it. Learn what you have to do to be worthy of the job. (Or go back and reread the *Back Up Your Lies With the Truth* chapter).

Most importantly, you should know that YOU are not alone. Everybody feels screwed up, at different times.

But stop worrying. Your secret is safe with me.

IT'S ALWAYS ABOUT YOU:

Are you afraid you can't do what is being asked of you? Do you feel insecure sometimes? Do you feel "over your head?" Everybody feels that way, at times. The feeling will pass. You are in this position because somebody, above you, believes in you. Even if that somebody hasn't even met you, YOU have to keep believing in yourself. Never give that up. If you are in charge, you will have to make some tough decisions. And keep in mind, most decisions can be reversed; even the really big juicy ones. So, the stakes aren't as high as they seem. Stick with it. Stick it out. Stay the course. Keep a stiff upper lip. Keep your nose to the grindstone. Keep you head in the game...*and* please hurry up before I run out of perseverance cliches.

And finally, remember how you promised me you would stay self absorbed throughout this book? Try using that attitude in your life, from now on. You matter to you. And the way you feel about yourself rubs off on everyone around you. And when you get frustrated at the crossroads of an important decision, listen to your gut first; regardless of what somebody else has in mind for you.

Trust yourself.

Stay true to yourself.

Consider *that* to be your supreme responsibility.

YOUR STORIES ARE NEEDED.

Enough about me, I'd like to know how *YOU* are doing. I would love to know what you found helpful or inspiring about this book. More importantly, if you have additional stories, examples, or nightmares you would like to share with our readers, please email them to me through my web site at: www.RossShafer.com.

I hope to hear from you,

Ross

ISBN 155395658-3